Cat Attacks

*True Stories
and Hard Lessons
from Cougar
Country*

Cat Attacks

Jo Deurbrouck & Dean Miller

SASQUATCH BOOKS
SEATTLE

Published by Sasquatch Books
Printed in the United States of America
Distributed in Canada by Raincoast Books, Ltd.
07 06 05 04 03 02 01   6 5 4 3 2 1

Cover and interior design: Karen Schober
Cover photograph: ©David A. Northcott/CORBIS
Back cover photograph: Brian Morris
Interior photographs: All interior photographs by Jo Deurbrouck and Dean Miller
except when noted otherwise.
Copy editor: Julie Van Pelt

Library of Congress Cataloging in Publication Data
Deurbrouck, Jo.
    Cat Attacks : true stories and hard lessons from cougar country / Jo Deurbrouck and Dean Miller.
    p. cm.
Includes bibliographical references (p.).
ISBN 1-57061-289-7
1. Puma attacks--North America. 2. Puma. I. Miller, Dean, 1961- II. Title.
QL737.C23 D48 2001
599.75'241566--dc21   00-052265

Sasquatch Books
615 Second Avenue Seattle, Washington 98104
(206) 467-4300
www.SasquatchBooks.com
books@SasquatchBooks.com

This book is dedicated to the people whose stories fill its pages and to those who helped us tell them.

Contents

Introduction

*"Mountain lions are indeed back. The question is:
Can we make room for them?"*
—Maurice Hornocker, biologist

*"Anything that makes people value an animal for what it is, rather
than for our fantasy of what it is, the better it is for the animal."*
—Sarah Durant, biologist

On January 14, 1991, in Idaho Springs, Colorado, an eighteen-year-old high school athlete went jogging on a class break and never returned. Two days later, would-be rescuers found his shallow grave. They noted big, round paw prints crisscrossing the snow. They saw that Scott Lancaster's face had been chewed away, his scalp half peeled and internal organs removed. The young man had been killed and partially eaten by a mountain lion.

The mountain lion, also called cougar, puma, or simply lion, preys mostly on deer and is well equipped for the task. Its short jaws deliver a powerful bite and its long, athletic body allows it to leap 20 feet or more, swarm up trees, or cling like a burr to a bull elk's back. Once common from east coast to west, the lion now lives primarily in twelve western states and Canada, where it is far from endangered. Yet despite its killing efficiency and robust numbers, cougar attacks on humans were, until recently, so rare in the United States that it was easy to believe the big carnivores harmless.

Researcher Paul Beier, who compiled a much-cited list of cougar attacks in 1991, found record of only twelve U.S. attacks between 1890 and 1980. In the 1980s, Beier recorded eight more. That was still only a handful, but a handful that nearly doubled the century's total.

Researching this book, we learned that the 1990s experienced an even greater acceleration in attacks. In the nine years following Beier's study, starting with Scott Lancaster, thirty-seven people were attacked or killed in the United States. This was three times as many as in the entire previous century. In this country and Canada, fifty-three people were injured or killed by cougars between 1990 and 1999.

Attacks: A Growing Problem

Cougar attacks are increasing, but risk is not spread evenly across cougar country.

	1951–60	1981–90	1991–99
Arizona	0	2	1
California	0	2	7
Colorado	0	1	7
Idaho	0	0	1
Montana	0	2	8
Nevada	0	0	1
New Mexico	0	0	0
Oregon	0	0	0
Texas	1	3	1
Utah	0	0	1
Washington	0	0	8
Wyoming	0	0	0
Alberta	0	2	1
British Columbia	4	8	17
Total Attacks	5	20	53

*Source: Authors' survey of all attack reports 1990-1999, survey by
Paul Beier of all attack reports 1890-1990.*

Scott Lancaster's death marked other changes as well. Before Scott, all but one of those killed had been children. But Scott was a strong young man who had nevertheless been unable to save himself. Two-thirds of those killed by cougars in the 1990s were adults, all of whom presumably thought that, if necessary, they could fight off an animal closely related to the house cat.

Most cougar attacks before the 1990s occurred in Canada which, for Americans, is the Great White North, a land of trackless wilderness and fearsome creatures. Since 1990 however, more cougar attacks have occurred in the United States than in Canada.

Before the 1990s, the few fatal attacks that happened in the United States occurred in backwaters like Evaro, Montana, where in 1989 five-year-old Jake Gardipe was snatched off his tricycle as he played 60 feet from his house. The 52-pound juvenile cat dragged the boy into cover to feed. But Evaro was on an Indian reservation in a wilderness state. The little town's tragedy didn't threaten urban complacency.

During the 1990s however, half of those killed were attacked near urban areas in populous states. The town where Scott Lancaster lived is a suburb of smoggy, sprawling Denver. Forty-year-old Barbara Schoener lost her life on a popular running trail a 45-minute drive from Sacramento. High school counselor Iris Kenna was birdwatching in a state park in San Diego County, population more than 2.5 million. Ask these people's families if cougars concerned them before that day, and they would probably have said, "No, of course not. There are dangerous places, but these places are safe."

Consider this: Mountain lions are one of wildlife conservation's happiest success stories. They once lived across North America, but the predator-extermination campaigns of more than two centuries had, by the 1950s, nearly succeeded. Cougars were gone from the American East and Midwest and rarely seen in the West. Marginally protected for only four decades now, cougars have rebounded so dramatically that it's tempting to imagine they simply strolled from thicketed shadows. They've reclaimed the inhabitable remnants of their western range and begun a slow repopulating march eastward. At the same time, human numbers are increasing, especially in America's fastest growing region, the West. Never before have so many cougars lived side by side with so many humans.

The new relationship between cougars and people, although a victory for modern environmentalism, is uneasy. As cougars are glimpsed more frequently in backyards, on jogging trails, and near suburban schools, demands to once again kill large numbers of cats get louder. After each well-publicized attack, wildlife agents are inundated by calls. Some callers are afraid, some merely curious. Some are infuriated.

Wildlife agencies and cougar researchers are often bemused by the outcry. Yes, attacks are increasing, officials say, but they're still incredibly rare. Millions visited state parks or walked forest trails in 1998. Cougars injured nine. Officials ask us to consider how many hundreds, perhaps thousands of times cougars simply hid and watched humans pass during the same period. They remind us that cougars are in much more danger from humans than humans are from cougars.

But those who fear cougar attack rely on a logic managers and biologists need to understand: The statistics promising that your child or jogging spouse won't scream in a cat's jaws this afternoon mean nothing if the animal is actually there, waiting beside the trail. That humans kill thousands of cougars each year means even less.

It was this tangle of issues that sent us, a veteran political journalist and a freelance writer/outdoorswoman with an interest in natural history, on a two-year search for answers. We interviewed cougar hunters, researchers, and game managers. We talked with cougar lovers and cougar haters. We read every bit of research we could find. We met with attack victims, some whose faces are still twisted by scars. We collected information about every cougar attack reported in the 1990s. We also talked with people who have had bizarre cougar encounters and people who would pay money for the chance to see a cougar, just once, in the wild.

The book that resulted is about many things. It's about cougar attacks and about the people who lost, even though the odds were strongly in their favor. It is also about fear, and why the fact that we're *nearly* safe among cougars doesn't reassure everyone. It's about game managers with an impossible job: to provide for the public safety, satisfy ranchers and deer hunters, accommodate cougar hunters, placate animal rights activists, and preserve mountain lions.

If you live in one of the twelve western states or two Canadian provinces that have substantial cougar populations, it's a book about you. If you live in the American Midwest, South, or East, it's a book about how cougars may be coming to live with you and why that's something you should think about. But most of all, this book is about mountain lions and what makes them unique. This predator was resilient enough to survive a centuries-long eradication campaign undertaken by the species most adept at erasing other species. It is adaptable enough to exist at the edges of and even within North American cities. It sometimes sees us as meat.

We do not want to alarm you into demanding that cougars be exterminated. We very much want them to thrive. But ignoring the reality—that the animal is occasionally dangerous—seems unlikely to preserve the mountain lion in this shrinking world. He is hauntingly graceful. Self-sufficient. Fabulously wild. And sometimes deadly. The mountain lion's unique qualities will doom him—or force us, finally, to address one of modern environmentalism's most difficult questions: Can we share habitat with big, wild creatures, and ignore the rules those creatures live by? Can we continue to pretend, living side by side with such an effective predator, that we are never prey?

—*Jo Deurbrouck and Dean Miller*
Idaho Falls, Idaho

1
California's Rude Awakening

Barbara Schoener (far right) with family and friends. Barbara would later become California's most famous cougar attack victim.

Fog pooled in the valleys; low clouds pressed onto the hilltops. Cool, gray drizzle hung between. In another month, the hills outside Sacramento would bake into brown loaves, but on April 23, 1994, the trails were still soft red clay, pocked by horses' hooves and mottled with fluorescent green mosses. Spring leaves unrolled on the scrub oaks and smooth-trunked manzanita.

It was a beautiful morning to be jogging above the American River on the Western States Trail, but the three men didn't notice.

They ran, walked, shouted, and stopped to listen. Each had his own fears about what they might find.

The previous morning, a woman named Barbara Schoener had driven away from the house she shared with her husband and two children for a long trail run. When she didn't return, her husband Pete had come looking here, at Auburn Lake Trails. He found only her car. Twenty-five hours later, dozens of would-be rescuers had found no sign of her. It was as if vivacious Barbara Schoener had jogged off the planet.

Friends of Pete, these three weren't part of the official search team. Thirty-seven-year-old Russ Bravard, a tall, long-legged second-grade teacher, thought Pete's wife had probably tripped and fallen, injuring herself. He called as he ran, but he also scanned the trailsides carefully. She might be too weakened by the long, chilly night to respond.

Kurt Fox knew that Barbara worked with insurance companies, finding jobs for claimants who might otherwise continue to draw unemployment benefits. Sometimes, he'd been told, her clients didn't want work. Sometimes they got angry. He pictured the forty-year-old brunette dead by the side of the trail.

Ernie Flores, big-hearted father of five, accepted Kurt's logic, but he couldn't picture Pete Schoener's pretty wife not alive. In his mind, she had been abducted. The stocky volunteer fireman was looking for a bad guy to fight and a woman to save.

None of them knew Barbara well, but Ernie remembered being surprised when quiet Pete met an outgoing young woman who dressed sharp and smiled often. It seemed a funny match, but after a five-month courtship, the couple married. Ten years later, when Ernie saw her at parties his jogger friends put together, he thought the two were pretty much perfect.

Russ, Kurt, and Ernie specialized in extreme distance running. The sport, called ultra running, began in the late 1970s. Its afficionados are a tight fraternity who push their bodies far beyond marathon limits: some races are 100 miles long. Pete was one of theirs, and Barbara had recently finished her first ultra. Worse, she had disappeared from a trail all three trained on. Whatever had happened to her felt like a personal offense.

So at 7:00 A.M. the morning after Barbara disappeared, the three arrived at Auburn Lake Trails, a gated subdivision adjoining a cluster of foothill paths. They were met by orange-vested volunteers who told them to leave because search and rescue teams had the operation under control. The friends waited until nobody was watching, then slipped under the yellow crime scene tape strung across the trail and began running.

What to look for? Anything. They ran through the cold damp, peering off the edges of the trail, calling, "Barbara!" every few yards. Fuzzily through the clouds, they could hear blatting search helicopters crisscrossing the sky. They knew that search and rescue crews had been looking, on foot and on horseback, for most of the night. But the search and rescue volunteers weren't runners. They didn't know the trails like Barbara, like these three.

Kurt kept saying, "She knows this area. She didn't get lost. Somebody has to have done this."

Ernie couldn't stop the mind movies: her struggle with the attacker, her abduction. "We'll get this guy," he vowed. Despite the chill, he began to sweat.

Minutes later, the men stopped at Russ's yell to peer with him down a steep slope carpeted with last year's oak leaves. The big oaks screened sunlight, so the undergrowth was sparse. Only new, leafless poison oak shoots poked through the leaves. That made the visor, 50 feet below the trail, plainly visible. It was white and looked cheap, like something a person wouldn't wade through poison oak to retrieve. Was it trash or evidence?

The men walked slowly back along the trail, looking for a reason to care. They found it near a bend in the trail, still in sight of the visor: two gashes of disturbed soil, as though someone had run off the downhill side. The first was about 2 feet below the trail, the second a foot or two lower. If the person who made those marks had regained the trail later, there was no sign.

Russ walked until he again stood above the visor. The slope was so steep that the big, moss-slicked oak trees leaned outward. A cheap visor and two footprints, assuming that's what they were. This was a popular trail. What were the odds that these relics had anything to do with Barbara Schoener? All the same, he began edging downhill, careful of his footing and the poison oak.

The visor was flat foam with a knotted surgical tube strap. It had been white, but thin reddish stains smeared it now. Russ looked at the red clay visible where his jogging shoes had scuffed up leaves. He rubbed his thumbnail into the stains. Blood or mud? He didn't know what blood would look like on a visor. He looked again at the mud beneath his feet and decided. Someone had lost a hat in a sudden breeze and kept going. The visor in his hands had nothing to do with the missing woman and everything to do with his own paranoia. The stains were mud. Searchers had examined this section of trail many times in the hours Barbara had been missing. If the visor had mattered, they'd have picked it up.

But still. Still.

"It's nothing. Let's go," Kurt shouted down.

"Wait a minute." Still holding the visor, Russ scanned the hillside before him. He looked at the red stains again. Looked up. And hated what he saw.

It was the kind of lightweight water bottle runners carry, white plastic with a soft strap that fits snugly in the hand. Even if the owner didn't care about a $10 bottle, the water inside would be worth a scramble to someone on a long run.

Russ picked up the bottle and suddenly found he could believe Kurt's deadly scenarios. Not only that Barbara Schoener been murdered, but that he, Russ Bravard, like it or not, was about to find her. He was as sure of this as he had, moments before, been sure she was nowhere near.

He weighed bottle and visor in his hands. The bottle was full, heavy. The visor was insubstantial. He turned to scan the hillside for more clues. Was it his imagination, or were leaves disturbed in a path leading downhill from where he stood? It felt like he had to follow.

Ernie heard Russ's next words through a rustle of leaves and snapping twigs as he and Kurt half-walked, half-slid after the tall grade school teacher. What Ernie remembers hearing is, "Oh my God, oh my God, oh my God." What Russ remembers saying is a calm, "She's right here."

Three hundred feet below the trail, hidden behind a tree, Barbara Schoener's bare calves and jogging shoes stuck out from one side of a shallow grave. Her dark hair was barely visible on the other. Leaves and debris obscured the rest of her. Russ stared, thinking of the compulsion that had drawn him here, and tried not to make it into a ghost story or the hand of God. He heard Kurt and Ernie arrive, but didn't turn.

"She might still be alive," Ernie said, although he knew she wasn't. He bent to touch her ankle; he couldn't bring himself to remove any of the debris. Her skin felt cold, the flesh rigid.

"She's dead," he heard himself say.

"What do we do?"

"We need to tell search and rescue," Kurt said. "Ernie, you're an EMT, right?"

Ernie nodded.

"Then you stay here."

Ernie listened to the scrabble as Russ and Kurt struggled up to the trail. He was surprised by how soon the sounds faded, and how deep was the forest silence they left behind. A creek, out of sight below him, provided a masking hiss he hadn't noticed until now.

He found he felt best in an alert crouch, elbows bent. He tried to smooth his breathing so he could hear. He figured the killer was long gone, but what if he wasn't? He, Ernie, would make sure nobody messed with her anymore. He imagined getting his hands around the man's neck. That would feel good.

Then he heard a soft rustling, like carefully placed feet. He twisted toward the noise, heard it again. "That guy's still here," he thought. He was amazed to experience a sensation he'd always thought was a wives' tale: the hair rose on his arms and neck. But no killer strolled from the concealing brush, and there were no further sounds. Ernie didn't relax. He felt—unalone. Watched.

Fifteen taut minutes later, uniformed men arrived. Two escorted Ernie back to Auburn Lake Trails' water treatment plant. The plant had been the makeshift center of operations for the search for Barbara Schoener, and now was becoming headquarters for the investigation of her murder. The three runners were told they would be interrogated. The thought made them nervous. For the first time, they considered how policemen investigating a murder might look at what they'd done, sneaking past that yellow tape. But there was no interrogation. After hours of waiting, the three runners were abruptly released.

The drive home through gray rain was quiet. Even Ernie, usually garrulous, could find nothing to say. He felt dry and small, curled up inside himself.

Kurt called that afternoon. "They think it might've been a wild animal," he said.

"A wild—what kind?"

"A mountain lion."

Ernie didn't believe him. He had seen a grave. People put people in graves. The rage in his gut needed a target, and you couldn't hate an animal. Besides, this wasn't wilderness. Auburn Lake Trails, with its winding streets and large, tidy yards, was forty-five minutes from Sacramento. Alaska or Wyoming? Sure. Animal attacks happened there. But not here, adjacent to a cloistered suburb. Still, an animal attack *would* explain why the three had been released without questioning, something that had been bothering Ernie all afternoon.

That evening, local newscasters talked about a woman killed by a cougar. Ernie watched as many news shows as he could find. Each time he was less angry at the murderer he had imagined and more ready to accept a nonhuman killer. Each time he was more furious at what seemed sensationalized attempts to bolster TV ratings at the expense of a woman who'd had the bad luck to be killed in a flashy way. And each time he heard the word cougar, he felt a creeping chill, a memory of hair rising on his arms and neck that morning and of the sound of footsteps. If a mountain lion had killed Barbara Schoener, had it watched the three men as they stood over her? Had it seen Russ and Kurt depart, and calculated the new odds in its inscrutable brain? Had he been furious when he should have been afraid?

That night at dinner, Ernie, who hates losing control, felt himself slipping. His failure to save Barbara mixed with the confusion and relief of having no murderer to hate, of coming to grips instead with the thought of a cougar that probably knew his face, although he had not seen its. Then there was his growing understanding that none of them would be allowed to grieve in private, that the world was watching this—this spectacle.

Ernie felt an odd sensation familiar from other difficult moments: he seemed to rise from his body into a corner of the ceiling. From that vantage, he saw his healthy, safe family clustered about the table, sheltered by the intimate shadows of dusk. He watched Di and his kids go suddenly still. And he watched the face of the muscular, black-haired man at the head of the table fold into knots of anguish. The man's shoulders heaved and his head dropped into his hands. His sobbing was raw and loud. Ernie watched Di put one hand gently on the man's right arm. Ernie's two eldest sons rose from the table, silently approached their crying father, and touched their foreheads to his.

2

Profile of the Killer

IN MEMORY OF
BARBARA
BARSALOU SCHOENER
JUNE 26, 1953 TO APRIL 23, 1994
WHO WAS TAKEN FROM US BY A
MOUNTAIN LION NEAR THIS SITE.
SHE WILL BE GREATLY MISSED
BY HER FAMILY, FRIENDS AND
FELLOW RUNNERS.

*About one-hundred yards from this memorial plaque, Barbara Schoener
was killed by a cougar in April 1994.*

Like Ernie Flores, the first officials to stand over Barbara Schoener's
body saw what they expected to see: a murdered woman, face
down and partially concealed in a sloppy grave.

Homicide investigators began to remove the 4 to 6 inches of
debris that hid Barbara Schoener's corpse, twig by twig in order to
preserve evidence. They exposed one arm, wrenched behind her
back, palm up, as though she had died with it tied. Not yet visible
was the massive wound beside the left shoulder blade, through
which portions of lung, esophagus, stomach, kidney, liver, pancreas,

and spleen had been removed. Tousled hair disguised the fact that much of the woman's face was gone.

It took more than three hours of painstaking work to learn the truth: there was no murder to investigate. Barbara Schoener's killer had long teeth and powerful jaws that could drive those teeth into a woman's skull. It inflicted wounds that resembled knife slashes. It scraped debris onto its kill, leaving a 6-foot-wide swath of cleared dirt around the mound. It left behind tawny hairs. It ate flesh.

In the state's history, only two fatal lion attacks had been documented. Both happened in 1909, when a woman and child died of rabies after being bitten. In recent years, reports of nonfatal attacks were accumulating, but they were still such rare occurrences that most people "knew" mountain lions posed no threat. Californians were about to get a crash course in cougars. The animal was unique in the state for the protections voters had insisted it have. Now it had committed the act many pundits had said it never would.

The mountain lion's scientific name, *Puma concolor*, means cat of one color, and the mountain lion nearly is. Tawny gold, gray, or tan fur fades to cream on his belly. Cream and dark brown patch his face. Dark fur may stripe his back or tip his tail and ears.

Normally a solitary hunter of primarily deer, the mountain lion is one of North America's few large native carnivores and arguably its most efficient killer. Adult lions have been known to take healthy bull elk, weighing some 600 pounds and well armed with sharp hooves and a powerful kick. Bulls carry a rack of branched antlers that, alone, can weigh 40 pounds.

The mountain lion has retractable curved claws that arc together when flexed. Press harder and the claws curve further toward each other. The resulting grip is hard to break. The wounds can look like knife slashes, especially those inflicted by the huge fifth claw, the equivalent of a human thumbnail, which some call the meat hook. A large lion, weighing 150 pounds and measuring 8 feet from nose to tail tip, may have claws an inch long. Lions in excess of 200 pounds have been documented.

The thirty teeth of a lion say as clearly as any other part of its body that their owner is strictly a carnivore. The lion's four canines are conical, made to grab prey and to separate skeletal joints when feeding. The front teeth, called incisors, are small and spaced close. They remove hair and feathers and strip flesh from bone. Premolars and molars do not have flat chewing surfaces. Instead, they are sharply ridged to help the animal shear dense muscle tissue. Bulging cheek muscles and short, blocky jaws together deliver a bone-crunching bite.

Unlike wolves, which can afford to run larger prey to exhaustion before risking combat, the lion tires quickly. So it adds to its formidable strength and speed a tendency to hunt from ambush. The combination means that prey may not sense danger until the cougar has already either missed its leap or attached itself firmly to the animal's back. The same is true for the cougar's human victims, who typically catch no more than a glimpse of the cougar before it hits.

Professional trackers arrived at Auburn Lake Trails the next morning with specially trained lion hounds. It was the hunters' job to fill in as many details as rain and the tramping feet of searchers had left intact. Then it was their job to locate and kill the lion. Justice seemed to require it. The public would almost certainly demand it. It also seemed reasonable to assume that the cat might kill again, even though data to support that assumption is, even today, inconclusive.

Based on the trackers' reports, recent cougar research, and the story written on Barbara Schoener's body, this is what probably happened the last morning of the runner's life, and what happened to her killer in the days that followed.

Barbara drove through the manned gate of Auburn Lake Trails subdivision, naming a friend who lived there and dropping the visitor pass on her dashboard. You could get to the trailhead from outside the subdivision, but it took longer and Barbara liked to be efficient. She drove past big, daffodil-sparkled lawns, which in the next few hours would fill with children playing and adults washing cars, mowing lawns, or weeding gardens. Then she was past the houses and into dense oak forest.

Moments later, she parked her Intrepid at gate #3 and began her warm-up routine. She wore purple shorts, white Nikes, and a hooded purple sweatshirt. She slipped her car key into her shorts pocket, pulled a Fleet Feet visor over her short brown hair and thin white gloves over her lacquered pink nails, and began to jog. It was 8:00 A.M.

As she warmed, Barbara stripped off the sweatshirt and knotted it about her waist. The damp morning chill poured like water across her bare arms. Less than an hour into her run, she began to jog around a long, U-shaped curve that, at its apex, overlooked the American River far below and the rumpled hills stepping up from its far side. The distant river whispered in her ears.

Barbara was new to ultra running and enjoying it. Her first race had been only a month before. Perhaps as she rounded the corner, she remembered the Cool Canyon Run, remembered feeling strong near the end and urging her lagging, long-legged husband, "C'mon, Mr. P. Let's finish together." But Pete Schoener was nearly spent. "No, you go on. Don't wait for me," he'd gasped, and she'd pulled reluctantly ahead.

Or perhaps she simply concentrated on placing her feet. The previous night, after their son's Little League game, she and Pete had discussed this day. Andrew had another game, so Barbara would run alone. Protective of his wife, Pete had suggested a trail frequented almost exclusively by horseback riders and other runners, where she'd be unlikely to be harassed. The route would take her 17 miles to Brown's Bridge and back on the Western States Trail. Although Barbara knew the trail well, this was only her fourth long practice run alone. She wouldn't have wanted to twist an ankle so far from her car.

Somewhere in the first miles of that Saturday's run, Barbara

Schoener, 5 feet 8 inches and 140 pounds, attracted the attention of her killer. The female lion was two or three years old, the equivalent of a human teenager or young twenty-something, and weighed 82 pounds. A male cougar her age might have weighed 120. She measured less than 2 feet at the shoulder, shorter than a big golden retriever. But cougars are long-bodied: on hind legs, she could have stared Barbara in the eyes.

She didn't look like the mountain lions in calendar shots. Nearly all commercial mountain lion images are of captive cats, who can afford that tell-tale, sagging paunch. Wild lions can't. They are lean and strapped with muscle from their Popeye-like forelegs to their bulging haunches.

She had large, greenish eyes and a long tail held in a low J curve. She shadowed the woman from above, loping in the characteristic posture of the cougar, head thrust forward and motionless below high, rolling shoulder blades. Her long, powerful hind legs propelled her across the hillside so gracefully that her big paws seemed to skim the ground without pushing upon it. She was healthy and normal in every discernible way except one: in a forest full of deer, the lion's favored prey, she was about to kill a human.

Once aggressively hunted for bounties that rose as high as $50 per cougar in the 1950s, lions had been protected in California for decades. They are no longer rare in the foothills of the Sierras, a fact that might surprise many of the region's human residents, particularly since the animals are only occasionally sighted. One of the reasons for the lions' seeming invisibility is low population density. Since male territories and female ranges are so large, typically 20 to 60 square miles per cat, a forest "full" of lions is likely to hold only a few adults. A region that supports one thousand black bears, for instance, might hold an adult population of one hundred mountain lions.

Lions are primarily crepuscular, sleeping or resting near kills during the day and hunting at dawn and dusk. One study found that 90 percent of a cougar's movements occur in darkness, the hours humans tend to be indoors. This also decreases the odds of sightings.

Those who have been shadowed by lions report such slow, studied creeping that it seemed the cat didn't move at all, or a staring face so absolutely still that it was at first invisible among brush and leaves. Stillness can be followed by leaps or about-face retreats so fast that some observers report a blurring of the cat's limbs. The upshot? A cougar that doesn't want to be observed probably isn't going to be.

This all means that although cougars live in almost every western forest, desert, or canyonland that supports deer and offers cover from which to hunt, including more than 60 percent of California, few humans have reason to know it. Even committed cougar researchers seldom get to see the creatures they study unless they've captured one. And in a forest "full" of cougars, even a very skilled cougar hunter is unlikely to see more than tracks until his dogs bark one of the elusive cats up a tree.

Barbara Schoener may have been followed for a few minutes or several miles, the cat loping smoothly through the heavy manzanita

Short, powerful jaws and sharp teeth help make the cougar a formidable hunter.

and scrub oak above the trail, shadowing the human who moved slowly along it. As Barbara jogged around the American River overlook, the cat left her to shortcut the U-shaped bend. There, where the trail straightened north into brushy shadow, the cat waited. Perhaps at first she was motivated simply by a predator's curiosity. She had watched or followed people before, just as she examined deer scent when she crossed it, just as she stared intently at anything that moved, even when her belly was full.

Where the trail straightened north, Barbara reentered heavier brush. River sounds were still faint in her ears. The steep bank on her left was about 6 feet high. The hillside dropped just as steeply on her right. Lions frequently hunt steep slopes, tackling their prey from above, letting gravity add force to the all-important first impact. Brush screened the backtrail from the cat's view, so for the waiting cougar, the woman first reappeared as the sound of running feet. Then suddenly the runner was visible, only now for the first time, she ran directly away.

Maybe it was just that simple, but it's hard not to want an additional catalyst for the moment that followed, a reason that this lion attacked this woman at this place and time, when every cougar alive has probably passed up at least one such opportunity. If there was such a trigger—Barbara speeding her pace, or making a sound of discomfort as she landed awkwardly on a weak ankle, or perhaps something odd about the way she smelled—we'll never know. What we do know is that the prey was unaware, the lion's belly was not full, and she hunted for two. Her seven-week-old kitten was stashed nearby.

The cat's silent, running leap was well-timed. Barbara, lost in a runner's reverie, felt herself violently propelled downhill. She registered sharp pain in her shoulders and neck and a sudden staggering weight upon her back. She struggled to stay upright, but managed only a few stumbling steps before she fell. The cat rode her for 45 feet until they came to a stop against a fallen fir.

Mountain lions often miss prey, but a cat that can wrap its heavy forelegs about the neck or shoulders of a deer and bury its front claws in dense muscle probably can expect to succeed. Longtime houndsman Bob Wiesner puts it this way: "If a lion knocks them down, the prey doesn't get away."

The earmark of a cougar kill is its efficiency. Most cougars kill by biting deeply into the skull or neck, causing head trauma, rapid blood loss or suffocation. A few seem to have perfected a technique for redirecting a large animal's own panicked strength. The deer bolts as the cougar lands on its back. The cougar simultaneously yanks the big ungulate's head about, so that as the animal attempts to flee, it literally charges into its own breaking neck.

But Barbara Schoener was not a deer. She had arms that could reach behind her head, hands that could grab. She lacked the long, curved ungulate neck whose vulnerabilities the lion intimately understood. The typical deer killed by a lion has a few deep wounds, and little or no other damage until the lion begins to feed. But human victims like Barbara Schoener may be bitten dozens of times about the face, neck, torso, and especially the arms and hands, apparently in an effort to subdue them after the initial attack fails to. These bites can be severe: some of the gashes in Barbara's hands cut to the bone. A fingertip was found inside a bloody glove near her body.

However long it lasted, the battle probably occurred in silence. Contrary to the Hollywood image of the snarling, spitting, screaming mountain lion, the big cats' victims almost always report a silent charge and attack.

The story behind all those wounds, the story of what happened after the cat leaped upon Barbara's back is important. Since her death, other adults have fought lions, sometimes with bare hands, and lived. Did she have a chance to save herself, or was Barbara Schoener all but dead as soon as a hungry lion noticed her jogging slowly and alone on a forested trail?

Two versions of the moments following the cat's initial leap are worth describing. The official one, published in area newspapers after the attack and based on forensics and other evidence found at the site, is that after the stumbling slide downhill, Barbara rose and faced her attacker. Where Russ Bravard would later find her bloody visor, she fought with what she had, her hands. She received deep bites on both arms and hands, leaving her blood in the freshly broken branches of the fir at her back. Then she turned and fled downhill 25 feet before being overwhelmed again. The bite that probably ended her life was delivered from behind. It cracked her skull.

The second version belongs to a professional tracker and lion hunter who says he has examined at least two thousand cougar-killed deer and other animals. Reading the faint clues remaining on the slope two days after Barbara died, Dave Fjelline believes she never regained her feet after that first sliding fall, never even saw the animal that killed her. The cat straddled the woman as they came up against the downed tree, pinning her to the slick clay with one arm trapped beneath her. Barbara reached back with the other, trying to grab whatever clung there, or perhaps simply covering her damaged neck. Teeth and claws raked at her.

Fjelline believes that in that initial attack the lion bit deeply into Barbara's neck, ripping an artery. Arterial bleeding is fast and violent. Blood sprayed into the fir's branches. Blood loss, or perhaps the bite that fractured her skull, subdued the struggling victim. The cat dragged Barbara further from the trail. There, she chewed a hole into the woman's back, crunching through ribs and vertebrae, and began to feed on the dying woman's organs.

If the official version is correct, it may be that, fleeing in pain or panic, Barbara Schoener forfeited her life. Those who survive cougar attacks are, almost universally, those who stood their ground or whose companions did. But if Fjelline is right, Barbara never had a chance to fight. Anything she could have done to save her own life would have to have been done before she stepped from her car.

Fjelline's version sounds particularly gruesome: a dying woman who, in her last moments, may have known she was being eaten. Birdwatcher Iris Kenna, attacked by a cougar several months later in Southern California, may also have lived long enough to hear or see her killer, a few feet away, chewing on her detached scalp. Those are disturbing images for humans, who place a high value on compassion. Lions, however, are no more cruel than any predator. They simply can't afford compassion. They risk their lives every time they kill large game, and sometimes even when they kill smaller animals, porcupines for instance. And cougars must kill—alone, often, and well—simply to continue living.

After feeding, the female did what lions everywhere do with their kills: she buried what had been Barbara Schoener by raking forest-floor debris over the body with her wide, soft-padded feet. Approximately seventy-five searchers, some with dogs, combed the area from midafternoon Saturday until midnight. They traveled on horseback, foot, and mountain bike. They saw nothing.

Later that night, as the forest quieted, the cougar uncovered the body and moved it another 35 feet from the trail. This, too, cougars almost always do, sometimes dragging their kills hundreds of yards in search of a hiding spot and, perhaps, cool, meat-preserving shade. She probably brought her seven-week-old kitten to the kill. The hash of tiny punctures found on the dead woman's side may mark the antics of a playful infant. The mother fed again. Perhaps the infant did too; he was being weaned. Then the cat reburied what remained of Barbara Schoener.

When the sky lightened, she padded to the creek for water. Then she picked a hidden place nearby to digest her meal, play with her kitten, groom her short, dense fur with a sandpaper tongue, and wait out the day.

The next night, as Ernie Flores sobbed in the arms of his family, the drizzle that had grayed the sky all that day turned to rain. Water pooled in the footprints of people and other creatures. It accumulated in the slight depression from which Barbara's body had been pulled by investigators. Somewhere in the oak forest, the female and her kitten, her first or perhaps the last survivor of a more typical litter of three, waited out the rain. The kitten looked exactly like an oversized, speckled infant housecat. If he lived long enough to lose those spots and the porcelain blue eyes of infancy, he would be lucky indeed. The odds can be as low as one in four.

The female was hungry. Her most recent kill, still rich with life-giving meat, had disappeared. Although cougar mothers often stash several kills in an area, this female had no others. She needed to hunt. Her kitten was still too young to keep up. So she hid him in brush or a rocky slot. His job was to stay alive and evade predators in the darkness. Her job was to kill. If she succeeded, she would feed and return, or bring him to the meat.

That same night, telephone calls crisscrossed the region as houndsmen organized to search for the killer cat. In the days that followed, hairs found at the site were examined to verify that they belonged to a cougar. An autopsy was performed on Barbara Schoener. The clearest bite mark was photographed, measured, and compared to bite patterns from lion skulls. Lion teeth must work perfectly, so the dental variation found among humans doesn't exist. Even the rate of tooth wear in aging lions is predictable. Forensics experts decided, based on the bite and on tracks found at the scene, that the animal they were looking for was a mature female or an immature male.

During the nights, the cougar crisscrossed her territory, unsuccessfully hunting; during the days she was written about in newspapers across the country. She was the primary occupation of local California Fish and Game officials. Five trackers and their hounds, dogs capable of detecting a lion's scent in the air thirty minutes after it has passed or of catching lingering scent in a cat's tracks days later, mapped the area and began to hunt. A team of scientists were ready to conduct a necropsy, an autopsy of an animal, in the event the hunters succeeded. The scientists' goals would be to find an explanation for what seemed horribly aberrant cat behavior, and to make sure that the hunters had killed the right cat.

In addition to telephones, radios, vehicles, guns and dogs, the hunters had in their favor a knowledge of lions. Despite the vast, folded terrain, reaching high into the Sierras and down into cultivated farmland, this was no needle-in-a-haystack search. Dave Fjelline and his fellow hound hunters knew, for instance, that mountain lions almost always stay near kills and often revisit old kill sites, even when no food remains. Since adult lions are territorial, an adult found in the area could be viewed with suspicion. Although Fjelline and his hunters didn't know about the kitten, its existence played in their favor as well: lion mothers collapse their territories when kittens are young, staying in a smaller area where game and hiding spots are most available.

Fjelline and the other hunters were not particularly concerned for their safety, despite the fact that they hunted an animal that had killed a human. Conducted intelligently, a cougar hunt is simply not dangerous work. This is because cougars behave in ways that, in a human, would be called timid. They seem to abhor face-to-face confrontation. More important, it's a rare mountain lion that, with dogs howling on his trail, won't leap into a nearby tree. Many cougar hunters hunt with only one or two dogs, knowing an adult cougar could make short work of them all if it chose, knowing it almost certainly won't.

The lion hunters blocked out an area about a mile square, with the site of the killing at its approximate center and the American River for one side, a subdivision for another, and trails on the other two sides. They patrolled the perimeter, marking every cougar track that entered or left. They worked their way in.

The hunt was handicapped by rains that fell in the days that followed. Even a "cold-nosed" dog, one that gets excited about very old scent, won't get anything from a two-day old track filled with rainwater. And although lions generally stay near recent kills, this lion's kill had been taken.

As the days passed, the odds of finding the right animal were fading, particularly if the killer was a subadult male. Males too young to have established territories can wander huge distances. The odds of being able to prove that a cougar they killed was the right animal faded faster yet. The cougar's digestive tract would quickly eliminate the most obvious evidence. Other evidence, like human blood and skin snagged under its claws, would remain only a few days longer.

On Sunday, May 1, eight days after Barbara Schoener took her last run, Dave Fjelline crossed the first fresh cougar tracks any of the hunters had seen in days. The tracks were moving toward the kill site a quarter mile away. Fjelline had a feeling the hunters' luck had turned.

Cliff Wylie, walking along the Western States Trail, saw the tracks a few minutes later. Cliff followed until he reached the point where, he remembered, Barbara Schoener had been forced from the trail by her attacker. The tracks turned downhill there. Cliff's two dogs hauled excitedly on their leashes. They smelled cougar.

Nobody knows why cats return to kill sites, but it doesn't seem to be simply for food. Lions have been known to revisit kills so old that only a few scraps of bone and hair remain to mark the spot. There they renew "scratches," or scent markers. Or they pick up a bone and play with it. Cliff knew that the lion who turned toward the spot where Barbara Schoener had died was almost certainly the animal he was looking for. He unsnapped his dogs' leashes and the hounds bounded down the slope.

Minutes later, he stood at the base of a black oak 300 yards from where Barbara Schoener's body had been found, staring up at a female mountain lion 20 feet above his head. Dave Fjelline and houndsman John Nicholas had released their dogs on the track as well, so an unruly pack barked and scratched at the tree. Treed lions often seem to feel secure, lolling across a branch and blinking sleepily at the frantic dogs below. But this cat looked nervous, tail tip twitching, eyes darting as though seeking an escape route. Should Cliff shoot her before she dove from the tree? Had he given her every benefit of the doubt? He had killed plenty of lions, but all of California was watching the final scenes of this play. Would they accept the ending he was about to create?

Uncertain, he called Dave on his radio. She's treed but she's nervous, he told Dave. What should he do?

"Hey, you know what needs to be done," Dave replied. Thirty seconds later, a single shot cracked through the oak forest.

The necropsy confirmed it: this cat had killed Barbara Schoener. Material scraped from under the claws of the lion's right front paw was DNA tested and found to be human. Barbara Schoener, along with about 11 percent of the population, had this particular type of DNA.

Exhaustive tests were run in hopes of finding that this lion suffered from a disease, rabies maybe. But there would be no easy answers: she appeared normal. She was lactating, though. Officials knew this meant that somewhere near the spot where first Barbara and then the lion had died, a kitten now waited for death as well. Another search began. Three days later, the dehydrated, weakened kitten was found among a jumble of granite just above the Western States Trail, probably at the exact spot where his mother had hidden him on the morning she was killed.

He lives now in a zoo that Pete Schoener, craggy, solemn faced, sometimes visits with his children. His name is Willow.

The family also visits the daffodil- and wildflower-planted resting bench Pete and other runners built on that last, panoramic bend Barbara jogged around before she died. Andrew, now in his early teens, likes to collect salamanders from the creek and beetles and other bugs from the carefully-laid rock stairs below the memorial. He takes them home in glass jars.

Pete runs the trail or comes to sit on the bench. He tries to remember the way Barbara looked as she breezed out the door that last time. He has been careful not to ask too many questions about what happened here, on this trail, a few hours later. He draws comfort from the hope that Barbara didn't suffer, that she died quickly. He doesn't want to learn anything that might steal that comfort from him.

From the rough stone bench, Pete can stare out at the hills and down at the river. It's a peaceful, gentle-seeming place. Frequent breezes stir the leaves of the oak trees, and a whispery cool water sound wells and fades. Despite the horror of what happened to his wife, Pete knows this is not a dangerous place, as places go. He enjoys the view, remembers Barbara. He keeps a watchful eye on his children.

3
Too Close for Comfort

*Jim Mepham's unprecedented image of a cougar hunting in
Glacier National Park.*

By the time Barbara Schoener died in 1994, the frequency of
cougar attacks was clearly increasing. Since 1980, not a year had
passed without at least one. Cougar populations had finally
rebounded enough to show humans what coexistence with a large
predator would look like. But the dawning realization that this
big carnivore *will* kill people sometimes masks a more basic fact
of cougar-human coexistence: cougars kill to eat, and humans are
not their favorite meal.

Few cougar stories illustrate this fact as well as that of Montana wildlife photographer Jim Mepham, who put himself in harm's way one sunny spring day when harm, luckily, wasn't interested in him. A high school science teacher as well as a photographer, Jim Mepham lived with his young wife in East Glacier, a tiny Montana town tucked into the shoulder of Glacier National Park. The park is home to black bears, wilderness-loving grizzlies, and Jim's favorite subjects, mountain goats.

In 1992, spring came early. The promise of new green against cobalt sky made Jim want to visit his favorite goat spot, Walton Goat Lick in Glacier National Park. He dressed in a long-sleeved white T-shirt and light-colored khaki pants. The tall, intense photographer wanted to get close to mountain goats, and looking like one couldn't hurt. On his way out the door, he grabbed a few handfuls of film from the refrigerator and an expensive new lens he'd convinced his wife he needed, despite the hole it punched in their budget. The rest of his camera gear needed no packing: it always waited in a padded backpack in his truck.

By 11:00 A.M., he and fellow photographer Steve Torno stood a mile above the goat lick on a steep, shaley slope. A herd of about thirty goats grazed higher up. The animals' thick winter coats were cloud-white against the blue sky.

Jim Mepham was in heaven: he loved the goats' narrow profiles, their long, bearded faces, almond eyes, and lips curved into what would, on human faces, be gentle grins. He loved the way they danced on precise, tippy-toed hooves over ground that made him stumble and grab for handholds. He knew he was getting crisp images. He loved that, too, especially since *Montana Magazine* wanted a goat picture for its cover. And although this day's work was just off the highway, he loved the high, rocky crags that goats more typically frequent. Goats have a pretty good view of the world, he liked to tell people.

Glacier National Park is grizzly country. Anyone in his right mind is cautious around grizzlies, so the two men had a bear plan: If confronted, they wouldn't run away. They'd stand together and face the animal. Jim usually carried pepper spray, an aerosol bear deterrent, with which he would, if necessary, defend them both.

But Jim was sure the area's grizzlies were still hibernating. And as he parked the truck an hour before, he had seen goats just above the road and he was in a hurry to have the short hike done, to be shooting. So he had slipped an extra lens and a dozen rolls of film into his pockets, attached the beautiful new lens to a camera body, affixed both to the head of his tripod, and strode up Snowslide Gulch. Left behind was his camera pack. In a holster on its hip belt was the pepper spray.

Snowslide Gulch falls steeply from high country to the Middle Fork of the Flathead. At the river's edge, the gray cliffs of Walton Goat Lick bleed life-giving sodium, potassium, calcium, and magnesium. In order to replenish these minerals in their winter-worn bodies, every spring and summer the goats come. They come in such numbers that Highway 2 has been lined with chain link to guide them away from the road and into the specially built Snowslide Gulch goat underpass. Fence and underpass together concentrate goat traffic in the ravine until their trails lace the steep hillside. Wispy flags of white hair festoon the twiggy knapweed. To a goat photographer—or a predator—those trails and that hair present a nearly irresistible invitation.

Jim was comfortable shooting here: he visited Snowslide Gulch so often that his feet had memorized the loose shift of the steep hillside's shale. Over his shoulder he could see his red Nissan, parked beside the busy highway less than a half mile away. And he didn't have to be alert for grizzlies. So for an hour he shot, thinking of nothing but the clicking shutter and the slow grazing approach of the goats in his viewfinder.

When the herd stampeded, Jim's first reaction was bemusement: it was odd, he thought, that he and Steve had sparked a panicked flight that streamed downhill *toward* them. Luckily, the men stood at the base of a rock outcrop, its top several feet above their heads. Before the stampede, they'd been photographing goats right above them on that outcrop. Within moments, goats were leaping from and streaming around it, just missing the two men. Jim and Steve shrunk reflexively against the rock. But Jim's camera remained pointed at the goats.

That was why what happened next unfolded inside the rectangle of his viewfinder. The frame did not make the action less heart-thuddingly real, but perhaps it did create for Jim a reassuring illusion of distance.

What Jim saw was a nanny, running shoulder to shoulder with the herd, but made desperately alone by what rode her: a big tawny animal draped across her back like a muscular rug, head twisted to bury its teeth in her throat. The mountain lion seemed to Jim bigger, heavier, and more vital than the goat to which it clung.

By reflex, Jim tracked with his lens. But even the reflexes of an experienced photographer have limits: during the next ten seconds, his index finger did not once compress the shutter button, even though goat and lion passed so close that their images blurred. This was the fourth wild lion Jim had seen, the first near enough to photograph, and the most dramatic event that had ever unfolded in front of his camera. But he wasn't ready.

Fifty feet below, the goat's flight ended. The cat rode the crumpling form to the ground, and then lay across the nanny, teeth still buried in her flesh. Silently it waited. Slowly, and just as silently, her sweet, patient smile still in place, the goat died. Her comrades ran downslope for another 200 yards before slowing.

Although they could have assumed themselves in danger—they were interlopers, and meat lay before them on the ground—Jim and Steve didn't consider leaving. Jim knew the solitary mountain lion was seldom photographed in the wild. Most marketable cougar photos are of game farm captives. Jim's insistence on selling only images of wild animals puts him in a disadvantaged elite. The possibility that he might capture at least the end of this story on film nailed his feet to the slope.

Besides, Jim probably felt he *was* armed. True, he didn't have his bear spray or a gun, but he carried an invisible shield: the confidence of the species that invented those weapons. Autowinders quietly whirring, he and Steve exposed frame after frame.

Minutes passed before the lion released its hold on the limp white neck. Then it raised its head to stare up the steep slope. Its eyes seemed to seek Jim's through the viewfinder. Its lips curled deliberately back to reveal long, curved canines. Jim recognized with a shock that the threat was directed at himself and Steve and for the first time, felt a sickening moment of uncertainty. But then, as if its point were made, the big cat rose and stalked into some low brush.

The warning had been unmistakable. Proof of the animal's lethal skill lay crumpled below them. Besides, they were clearly forcing the lion from its meal. The men started picking their way back toward the truck.

The goats gradually began to browse once more. Jim began again to enjoy the windless, unseasonably warm air. Sunlight drew sparkling color from new green shoots, ruddy rock, white goats. Jim already regretted their decision. Why leave? There was no sign of the lion. It was probably returning to its kill now that the men had moved away. Hesitantly at first, but then with greater absorption, Jim and Steve began again to frame and snap goat images. One would later become the magazine cover Jim had hoped for.

Jim focused his attention on the original band of goats as they browsed up Snowslide Gulch toward a smaller, intersecting ravine. He also noticed a new nanny band of about five females and yearlings coming into sight a half mile away, picking their way down Snowslide Gulch. The nannies would cross the little, dry ravine. Jim and Steve began to work toward it as well.

Jim tried not to think about missing the priceless gift of those first, raw images. It had happened so fast that details were already fading, and he'd have no pictures to conjure them back. Even the memory of the cougar's silent warning couldn't stop him from wishing he could relive those moments. Neither could his concern that he and Steve had cost the nanny her life. If she and her band had, by watching the photographers, overlooked the greater danger, it was done and there was no changing it.

Many shots later, the men found themselves on a cliffy outcrop, brick red dulled by gray lichens. Thin plates and long, bloody shards broke under their boots. This outcrop topped one lip of the little ravine, about 100 yards above its intersection with Snowslide Creek. The new nanny band was now on the little draw's far side, almost in photo range. The men waited quietly.

Then Jim saw the lion. It was crouched at the edge of some alders. Like the men, it watched the little band. Its stillness and golden brown coloring made it nearly invisible. If Jim hadn't known a lion was near, he'd never have seen it, even when it began to move, its low-bellied stalk was so painstaking that the next five minutes brought it only 20 feet closer to the goats. It moved by gliding a few feet forward, freezing into a cat-shaped rock, and then gliding forward again.

The men knew they should go—they were way too close this time, barely 100 feet away. But instead, they balanced their tripods on the outcrop. Jim's heart pounded and his hands shook so hard that without the tripod he couldn't have worked. He was excited, however, not afraid. He was sure he was about to be given a second chance at the same, once-in-a-lifetime shot.

The goats grazed slowly toward the draw. The lion inched slowly toward the goats. If goats or lion were aware of the humans, neither gave any indication. Tension wound Jim's jaw muscles into aching tightness.

Finally, lion and goats were only 15 feet apart. Jim thought he could see the cat delicately tremble with tension. If the goats looked up, it would be in plain sight. The sure-footed animals would scatter and flee. But they didn't look up.

The lion uncoiled. In a single long bound it landed on a nanny, burying its face in her thick mane. The nanny leaped as if she had burst into flame, and then careened straight toward the two men. She struggled to keep her feet beneath her, as though she knew falling meant death. She threw head and shoulders from side to side, but didn't—or couldn't—hook her tormentor with her little black horns. *Click,* went Jim's shutter.

Without hesitation, the nanny charged off the ravine's 15-foot wall. Goat and cat flew, stretched necks and front legs pointing toward the ravine's floor. *Click.* They landed side by side, the goat crumpling as she hit. The cougar fell too, but rose immediately, dropping onto her and repeating the patient, throat-squeezing kill. Barely 20 feet from Jim, the scene filled his viewfinder. *Click.*

The goat's white hair was unstained by her dying. Jim heard no growls, no piteous cries, no sounds of struggle, only the anxious scrambling of the remaining goats, the trickling creek in its steep, waterfalled course, the irrelevant sound of cars on the highway, and the whir of his motor drive. He rewound and reloaded once, wincing at the noise. *Click. Click. Click.*

As he shot, Jim's excitement again gave way to uncertainty. Before the lion's leap, the men had been separated from danger by a cliff and the little dry ravine, and the photographers had still felt uneasily close. Now only a few yards of thin air and the rock upon which they stood separated them and the powerful predator. And although cougars are thought to prefer to attack from hiding and from above, as this one twice had, they are also known to be capable of leaps in excess of 15 feet. "Maybe we should leave soon," Jim thought. *Click.*

Then the cat raised its head, stared at the photographers, and parted its jaws. It rose, teeth visible, and padded slowly to the base of the rock. Fifteen feet above its silent snarl, Jim suddenly felt more terrified than he'd ever been in his life. He also realized he was alone. Without noting it, he'd been hearing for several moments the clattering rocks and snapping brush that marked Steve's rapid retreat.

Amazed at his foolhardiness, dispassionately noting that his knees had begun to actually bang together, Jim shot frame after frame of the cougar's upturned snarl. The pacing cat seemed to measure the scant distance that separated them. The message was clear: Jim was invited to leave. But he couldn't stop shooting. He'd never seen pictures like the ones he was getting.

Then the lion swung away and began to loop around the left curve of the outcrop. For a moment Jim was relieved. Then he knew, as clearly as if the cat had spoken its intentions, that in moments it would reappear on the hillside behind him. It would claim the advantage of higher ground. It would stand between Jim and the red Nissan truck, which in the corner of his eye suddenly looked toylike and impossibly distant.

Clarity struck: This was not about photographs. It was about living or dying. It had been all along for the other participants and now it was for him as well.

Jim grasped the heavy Boden tripod by its feet. This created a weapon four feet long; at its business end was his new $2,000 lens on his favorite Nikon camera body. He thought that, with luck, he'd get one good swing. A tiny corner of his mind occupied itself imagining how he'd explain to his wife that he'd broken the new lens on its first trip out. This reaction was not one he'd have guessed would precede bloody combat.

Then he fled backward, tripod extended toward the outcrop, stumbling across the steep slope.

He was 25 yards away when the cat looped back into view. At this moment, Jim's lion encounter became exactly like the vast majority of frightening lion encounters. The animal had just demonstrated an easy and lethal prowess. It was hunting and obviously intent on creating more meat than it could immediately consume. Jim stumbled, unarmed, backward along the same unstable slope which had helped the cougar tackle and kill the first goat. Yet the cat did not follow.

Instead, it stepped onto the crumbly red outcrop and placed its big paws where Jim's feet had been moments before. Its ears, which had been low, rose straight from its small, round head. Its jaws were neatly closed. But its eyes did not release him. Again, the message seemed clear: Leave right now. Or else. This time, Jim knew he would accept the invitation.

4
Vancouver Island,
the Original Hotspot

Royalty and movie stars visit Victoria's opulent Empress Hotel.
So did a cougar in 1992.

When startling encounters began to make news in America in the 1980s, baffled officials searched for advice on a mountainous island chipped off Canada's west coast. Almost half of all cougar attacks between 1890 and 1990 occurred on this tiny patch of forest little bigger than Vermont. In the last ten years, Vancouver Island has still accounted for more than a third of all attacks. And although half of a century's cougar victims is still a small group, thirty-seven to be exact, almost everyone on the island has a good cougar story to tell.

Glenn Galbraith has three. He saw two cats up close in the 1980s when he was working at a pulp mill in one of the small timber towns on the northwest coast. Both times, he was jogging and surprised the cats, which ran away. Another time, Galbraith was driving to work when the car ahead slowed, presumably for a bicyclist pedaling down the shoulder. The real cause of the slow-down became clear when a golden shape flew from the brush behind the cyclist, wriggling and pawing the air during its impressive hang-time. The cougar landed in the far lane and disappeared into the ditch. The driver ahead of Galbraith later said the cougar had chased the bicycle's rear tire for 100 yards before the dramatic leap witnessed by Galbraith. The cyclist witnessed nothing at all. He was startled to learn that he had had company.

Vancouver Island's best cougar stories aren't always the newest ones. One night in 1951, a sixty-three-year-old telephone line worker far up the island's east coast saw a cougar pacing outside his cabin. When Eddie McLean turned off his gas lantern at about 9:00 P.M., the cougar crashed through the cabin window. McLean struggled with the animal in the dark, found his knife and slashed at it. Breaking free, McLean fled in his underwear, climbed into a rowboat, and rowed 5 miles to another cabin. He was found the next morning, weak from blood loss and exposure. The cat was later discovered on McLean's bed, according to newspaper and wildlife agency reports.

Across the island and further south, fishing and tourist villages line the coast that faces the Canadian mainland. Lush flower baskets hang from eaves, and highway signs invite passersby right into the homes of sculptors, potters, and weavers. One of those villages is Campbell River, where Karen Stevan and her partner were awakened one August morning at 1:00 A.M. by their housecat, Little Joe, screaming through the pet door. The cat was shivering and yowling, so they comforted it and finally got back to sleep. When they awoke the next morning, there were seven cougar-killed sheep in the pasture of the farm where they lived. Karen found a deep scratch on the cat's back. Little Joe, it turned out, had been a very lucky cat that night.

At the southern tip of the island lies elegant Victoria, provincial capital of British Columbia. Folks there may wear suits, ties, and cellphones, but they've got the most famous cougar story of all.

It was mid-March of 1992 and Tim Loewen was minding the yellow cashier's booth in the Empress Hotel's underground parking garage. The TV was on and he was talking on the phone, so he barely noticed the car at the gate until the cabby honked. Tim cupped the phone and slid open the window.

"You got a cougar in here," the cabby hollered, pointing down the ramp into the concrete cavern.

"What?" Loewen said with a laugh.

"A cougar just walked into your parkade," the cabby repeated.

The Empress is no rustic lodge in the woods. It's a seven-story castle in downtown Victoria where the bellmen dress in livery, the staff's manners are spot-on, and the best room fetches $1,500 Canadian per night. A city block wide, it's the focal point of the teeming inner harbor. More than 100,000 pilgrims a year come for high tea at the Empress. Just as Queen Elizabeth once did, they poke out their pinkies, hoist a dainty china cup, and wait for the "Tea Mum" to serve a scone or some clotted cream.

A cougar here? Just in case, Tim closed the security gates. About then, a big golden animal walked up out of the gloom, passed Tim's booth and leaped against the gate. Tim was in awe. The cougar moved with the grace of a dancer and looked like it was all muscle.

When Tim called upstairs to ask what he should do, night manager David Woodward figured some nervous part-timer had been spooked by a stray dog. Still, one had to take precautions. It wouldn't do to lose a hotel guest to a wild animal.

Feeling a bit silly, he dispatched bellmen to seal off all doors into the garage. Then he went to see for himself. Two levels down, he and the valet van driver he'd grabbed found no cougar. There was a smartly dressed guest putting a bag in his car. A little drunk, the man laughed uproariously at Woodward's warning. A cougar among the Cadillacs? It sounded funny to Woodward, too. Driving on, Woodward leaned out the window to warn a woman rummaging in her car trunk. She didn't laugh, though: He didn't get far past the word "cougar" before she slammed the lid and bolted for the elevator. Woodward and the driver were still chuckling when something big glided through the van's headlights. Fire? Woodward knew what to do. Earthquake? It was right there in the emergency procedures manual. Cougar in your three-hundred–car garage? Not a clue. He left to make a plan.

The call from the Empress was a relief to conservation officer Bob Smirl. For two days, reports had traced a cougar traveling first through Victoria's suburbs, then deeper and deeper into the city. One of those reports had troubled him. The cat had walked right past a restaurant owner cleaning his parking lot with a high-pressure hose. The animal sounded a little too bold to Smirl and he was glad it was finally penned up, even if the pen was the Empress garage.

At the hotel, the first thing Smirl saw was a crowd of two hundred people, including what looked like every television and newspaper reporter in town, peering into the garage through a steel security grate.

Smirl carried a tranquilizer gun, plan A. His houndsman and a helper each held a dog on a short leash. The houndsman was also in charge of plan B: a 30-30 Winchester carbine. Somebody raised the grate. Smirl and the others stepped inside. The gate closed behind them with a metallic crash.

"Ok, now we're locked in here with this thing," Smirl thought. The crowd murmured outside. It sounded like they were rooting for the cougar.

The dogs seemed to strike fresh scent everywhere; their baying echoed through the cavernous parkade. Smirl eyed the rows of late-model luxury sedans: Mercedes-Benzes and Cadillacs. "How am I going to explain bullet holes in these cars?" he wondered.

Moments later, the cat stepped from behind a small car directly into their path. Ears back and eyes slit, it crouched, then began to belly-crawl toward the dogs like a tabby toward a robin.

The frantic hounds tried to lunge at the cougar. Their handlers leaned back hard. Bob eased to the side, looking for his shot. Intent on the dogs, the cat didn't notice him until the fluffy-tailed metal dart found the animal's hip. Then the trapped cougar spun fast and locked eyes with Bob. Bob raised the dart gun before his face and chest, and braced for impact, but the cougar spun away instead, diving into a dark corner under an air duct. A second dart knocked the cat out.

The crowd cheered when Smirl and his helpers carried out the cougar, handcuffed in case it woke too soon. This was perfect P.R., Smirl thought. Cougar stories ending with a game warden's bullet were not nearly as popular around Victoria as in the little bush towns up-island. He showed people the animal's claws and teeth as it lay on his tailgate. He answered questions about where the cat would be released. Then he placed a towel over the cougar's head to make sure it stayed unaware, and fifty people, one by one, quietly filed by to touch it. One woman snuggled her face into the soft fur of its belly.

"Thank you," she told Smirl. "This is the most wonderful experience I've ever had."

When he was interviewed on the nationwide news by the CBC, night manager Woodward joked that the cougar was a bit late for tea, and not dressed for it anyway. Almost a decade later, a picture still hangs in the Empress's lushly carpeted, richly furnished lobby: a limp mountain lion being evicted from the hotel.

The Empress cougar made for a wonderful story, but it also raised an interesting point. Everywhere except Vancouver Island, it seems, if you were to fly over the scenes of in-town cougar sightings, you could trace a leafy path from forest to town, perhaps a wooded riverbank or greenbelt. The cougar that appears amidst city traffic has simply followed familiar habitat until it pops up inside our concrete and asphalt world. But the Empress cougar must have crossed miles of pavement, and it isn't the only cat that has. The cougar that wandered into Craig Grebicki's downtown Victoria office one fall day in 1998 did the same thing. There is no wide river corridor or greenbelt that could have led either cat so far into Victoria unawares. These cats were bold.

Craig is a salesman for a fishing gear manufacturer in James Bay, a crowded older neighborhood overlooking Victoria's harbor. It was a hot afternoon, so someone had left open the front door to the building.

Just as he was getting ready to take a break from the phone, the tip of a long tail flashed in the corner of Craig's eye. He caught his breath when the animal reared up to place its paws on a window sill: it was a cougar. All that stood between Craig and the cat was a file cabinet and a potted plant.

The cougar ignored him and dropped back to the floor. Then it walked into another office. Through a window in the wall, they made eye contact for three long seconds. When the cougar turned away, Craig was ready: he shoved his chair into the open doorway and sprinted for the exit. He heard something thud against the door as it slammed shut behind him.

If a near-town study were ever funded, Dr. David Shackleton believes that researchers would find Vancouver Island cougars regularly pass through cities and towns. One of his graduate students in the University of British Columbia wildlife program tracked a radio-collared cougar from the wild heart of the island straight through Nanaimo, population 85,000. When it reached the busy waterfront, the cougar jumped in and swam 4 miles through the ferry lane to built-up Gabriola Island, where 4,500 people live.

Maurice Hornocker, the grand old man of cougar research, believes Vancouver Island cougars are unusually bold and aggressive. He has challenged researchers to explain why Vancouver Island cougars don't behave like those in Santa Clara County, California, and on the Olympic Peninsula of Washington State, where mountain lion populations are also dense.

Hornocker thinks intensive hunting may have increased the proportion of aggressive cats on the island. The idea is that hunting weeds out shyer cougars, which tree quickly and therefore are easier to kill. Aggressive cats stay on the ground to fight or elude the dogs. They survive, breed, and pass on aggressive habits or genes.

Houndsmen killed as many as 460 cats per year on Vancouver Island in years past, a staggering number when you consider that biologists think 1,000 cougars live there. Even today, it's thought that hunters kill 15 percent of the island's cats every year. If it's true that an island ecosystem, because it experiences no immigration, tends to concentrate the effects of changes in the gene pool, Vancouver Island hunters may have spent the last century shaping a bolder, more aggressive cougar.

And, if you listen to Doug Janz, chief of the Ministry of Environment's wildlife division on Vancouver Island, the townsfolk then set out a welcome mat. From the craggy roadside overlooks just north of Victoria it can appear that the island's center is an undisturbed sanctuary of deep timber. But from the air, Vancouver Island is a checkerboard of clearcuts. It took settlers one hundred years to cut one third of the old growth. The second third was shaved off in only thirty. In a few generations, cougars and other wildlife have adapted to poor habitat in second-growth plantations, or have moved near sprawling towns. They had to. On an island, there's no place to run.

Doug Janz says that these days, some of the island's healthiest deer herds live near towns on the east and south coasts, where most of the people live as well. What Janz calls "rosebush deer" live well on lawns, flower beds, fairways, and hobby farms. He believes cougars have moved in to hunt those deer.

"The golf courses and greenways are little green magnets," Janz says. "Opportunities for meetings [with humans] are increased."

Vancouver Islanders say encounters and attacks are more frequent because there are more cougars on the island than anywhere else in the world. They say it with rueful relish, the way New Yorkers brag about how expensive rents are.

It might be true. A research team on the east side of the island once counted three times as many cougars as is typical elsewhere in North America. But that's all that's unusual, says Matt Austin, the province's large carnivore specialist. Vancouver Island cougar attacks are still so rare as to be little more than random collisions of bad luck and bad timing, he argues.

Even so, Vancouver Island may show Americans the shape of things to come. Cougar numbers have rebounded in the United States. Some regions in the states now have cougar densities not much lower than this little island, home to 700,000 humans, 1,000 cougars and three dozen collisions of bad luck and bad timing since 1914.

5

A Father's Nightmare

<figure>Photo courtesy of John and Joan Musselman</figure>

*The Musselmans: John, Kyle, Brittany, Brad, and Joan,
six months before a cougar attacked Kyle.*

Carved into a forested Vancouver Island hillside that overlooks
the village of Gold River, Scout Lake could be any of a thousand
middle-class subdivisions of Seattle, San Francisco, or Denver.
Sidewalks, streetlights, and molded gutters march alongside the
asphalt with comforting regularity. There are no rickety power-
lines overhead. New cars and speedboats wait in the carports of
well-tended two-story homes. The only difference is this suburb's
commuters work in the bush and the nearest city is three hours
away. The woods stretch from the edge of town for miles in all

directions, a veritable ocean of trees.

May 9, 1994 dawned unusually sunny for spring on the north end of Vancouver Island. Cool, rich air poured off the surrounding mountains. In a yellow house midway along Donner Street, twelve-year-old Brad Musselman began the task of rousing his seven-year-old brother, who shared the basement with him. Kyle, who let his gung-ho sister Brittany do more than her share of the chores, was also mostly willing to let Brad be boss. Kyle dressed in jeans, sneakers, and a checkered flannel shirt. In his pockets, he hid a pair of tree-shaped car air fresheners he'd been carrying around for weeks. One was vanilla, the other, pine. Brad laughed every time Kyle explained he liked to smell fresh.

Brad herded Kyle upstairs for breakfast. As usual, eight-year-old Brittany was already up. Their father, John, a late-shift mechanic for one of the logging outfits that supplied the pulp mill, was making breakfast. Their mother, Joan, an EMT, was away at a logging camp on Quadra Island, accessible only by plane.

They ate looking out the bay window at miles of green timber, the reason for this town. Then they settled in front of the TV to watch the Mario Brothers "Hoo! Hoo!" through another episode. At about 8:30, the children slung up their day packs, said a quick goodbye to their dad, and left for school. John went back to bed.

At the corner of Donner and Cala they met Tony Olsen and his older brother, Jamie. Farther up Donner, where trees were rapidly refilling unsold home lots, a 100-foot staircase ran down the forested hillside from Scout Lake subdivision to the school. Paved with railroad ties, gravel, and asphalt, it dropped three flights, with long asphalt landings between. An alder thicket grew on either side of the eight-foot path. Just past the bottom step, Canadian Highway 28 turned into a gravel road. The school lay straight across the highway.

Kyle's and Tony's oversized backpacks bounced back and forth across their butts as they clattered down the stairs one landing ahead of Brad and Jamie. Brittany dawdled behind. When Tony called out a race and took off, Kyle shouted and chased after him.

Suddenly, a dark blur burst out of the alder thicket and flew after Kyle. Stretched out in midair, the lunging animal seemed to Brad as long as the staircase was wide. Then its front paws found Kyle's right shoulder. The impact spun Kyle around and slammed him onto his back, looking up into the jaws of the golden animal that completely covered him.

"Holy shit, it's a cougar," Brad said.

Kyle began screaming in short, high-pitched bursts louder than any kid Brad had ever heard. He kicked at the cat's belly and tried to hold its jaws away with chubby hands. The cougar was swiping at him with its front paws and lunging to bite his face.

Tony Olsen had stopped when he heard Kyle's first screams. Now he was throwing rocks at the cat. Brad didn't bother with rocks. They needed an adult. With his brother still screaming on the ground, Brad sprinted for home.

John woke the moment the door banged. As he struggled from bed he heard Brad's voice, cracking as it rose. "Dad, hurry! Kyle's being attacked."

He scooped up a pair of Levi shorts from the floor and plunged down the stairs two at a time.

"Dad, hurry up, he's being eaten by a cougar!"

"What?" John yelled back, fully awake now and staring at only two of his three children. "Where?"

Their eyes were huge. "On the stairwell! Hurry up!"

The top of the stair was three hundred paces from his door. "Oh my God, a cougar," John thought, as he ran barefoot up the street. He could see the staircase, but he wasn't getting there fast enough. "This isn't really happening."

John had hunted and hiked the hills of British Columbia all his life, but he had never seen a cougar in the wild. Paved, suburban Donner Street was nothing like the muddy trail he'd walked to school as a boy on the mainland. Here he was, running past the doctor's house and the piano teacher's living room to face a cougar. All he could hear was his feet slapping the pavement and Kyle's little house-dog, Dexter, scratching along behind him. "There's nobody out here," he realized with a start. "We're going to need some help here."

When he grabbed the railing and made the turn onto the staircase, he spotted a neighbor woman in a housecoat throwing a palm-sized rock into the alders beside the stairs. After the kids had come screaming past her house, Ingrid Dahl had watched another woman run for the phone and realized a child was alone down there. She had hurried to the top of the staircase dressed in ballet slippers and her husband's blue bathrobe and called out "Where are you?" Far below her, beside the last landing, she could see alders wildly whipping. She hurried down the steps, but her imagination slowed and finally stopped her.

"Where is he?" a voice demanded from behind her. "Where is he?" and she pointed, faint with relief.

Running past her, John Musselman crouched down until he spotted Kyle's sneakers. He bent closer. His eyes moved methodically from the boy's feet to his legs. No motion. Kyle lay on his stomach. As John crawled closer, something inexplicable happened: the boy's body slithered away, rippling like water over the rocks.

John startled and then crouched lower to see where Kyle went. Kyle's feet bounced away through a leafy tunnel and came to a stop 20 feet away. John's eyes finally took in the boy's torso. Slowly panning, almost forcing his eyes to move, he saw that Kyle's arced-up back and twisted neck were yanked up off the ground by the cougar.

Its jaws closed over Kyle's face, so that cougar and boy were mouth to mouth. The cat was crouched slightly to the left of Kyle's body. Hanging from Kyle's bloody white skull was most of his scalp, a wet, hairy mop coated with leaves and dirt. Kyle wasn't moving. He had to be gone. John and the cougar locked eyes. The cat's tense posture and gaze said, "This is mine."

"You son of a bitch," John muttered. He glared harder. So did the cat. A long moment passed. John suddenly boiled with fury.

"Kyle's had enough. He ain't going to go through any more."

He bared his teeth and roared, "Get off him!" The cat flinched, but didn't drop the body. Instead, it hunkered even lower. John charged, intending to either retrieve his son or dive in beside him.

"Get off him!" he shouted again, raising his arms to grab the cat or fend it off. The last shout seemed to break the cat's trance. Just as John closed the gap, the cat dropped Kyle and leaped, not at John, but four feet above his outstretched arms. The cougar landed, spun, and dashed into the bush. John yelled again to make sure it kept moving. Then he turned to his son.

Kyle was lying face-down with his arms outstretched like a crucifix. John could see slick, bloody skull bone on the crown of Kyle's head. At the base of the skull was a little tuft of unbloodied blonde hair and then the sweet pale skin of his neck. Supporting the neck the way he'd been taught in first-aid classes, he turned the boy over. At the sight of Kyle's face, he gasped and nearly dropped him, bobbling the head and shoulder in his hands.

The face was all blood and raw flesh. Only the tip of a nose remained, with nostrils holding it to the head. The bridge of the nose was gone. John could see into the nasal cavity. Both cheeks were shredded, the skin turned inside out to reveal muscles and bone. The mouth was ripped apart. A tooth or claw had torn the flesh from temple to ear. John could see a mostly empty eye socket and a flattened eyeball. The ear on that side was ripped. John couldn't find any sign of the little boy whose face had crumpled into tears two weeks before when his dad had questioned him about goofing around with those damn air fresheners under his arms.

"Oh my God," John breathed. Dexter shouldered in beside him, trying to nuzzle the boy. John shoved him away.

Then a little bubble of blood formed where the boy's mouth should have been. John snapped to attention.

"Kyle!" he called out sharply. "Hang in there! Kyle, it's Daddy! Breathe! Breathe, Kyle! Just breathe! Don't worry about anything, just breathe!"

Standing up, John made his way toward the path, trying with one hand to throw Kyle's scalp back up on his head when it caught on branches. "Kyle, breathe. Do nothing but breathe," he said. He didn't know what Kyle could hear, but it made him feel better to say it.

And then he stopped. Kyle had said something. John was sure of it.

"What?"

"Who are you?" faint and quiet like it took all the boy's effort.

"Kyle? . . . Daddy! Just hang in there."

And then hope hit him, hard. All those head wounds, yet Kyle had spoken.

"Kyle, are you OK?" he asked.

"No," whimpered the boy inside the mash of blood and bone. "No."

"Just hang in there, Kyle. You're going to be OK. Don't do anything but breathe."

His across-the-street neighbor, Glen McNichol, carrying a homemade knife the size of a machete, practically ran into them as they emerged from the bush.

"He's alive," John said. The men ran toward the school.

In the teachers' parking lot, a red Ford minivan was easing into place. The driver looked up when John yelled from the last flight of steps.

"Cougar attack! I need help. Cougar attack!"

"Open the back door," teacher Carol Volk told her daughter. "You don't have to look. A child is hurt."

John cradled Kyle as they drove, repeating over and over, "I'm here . . . Hang on, I'm here with you . . . Breathe."

He burst into the Gold River clinic with Kyle in his arms. "Cougar attack, cougar attack! He's alive!" he shouted, willing it to still be true.

In the emergency room, a nurse asked as she cut off Kyle's bloody shirt, and pants and untied his sneakers. "Do you want these back?" "No," John said, shaking his head. "What's he weigh?"

the doctor asked, calculating a sedative dose. John had no idea.

A Bowater Paper Company helicopter arrived to take Kyle to the nearest hospital in Campbell River, an hour away by car. "If you want to do anything for Daddy, breathe," John commanded as they were loading Kyle into the chopper. "Breathe."

The pilot shot a thumbs-up and John shot one back. John had gotten to Kyle in time and the boy was breathing just like he'd been told. Now that he was in expert hands, the worst was over. The helicopter spun up and one of the doctors, a next-door neighbor, drove John home to get cleaned up and dressed for the trip to Campbell River.

In his bathroom, John left bloody fingerprints on everything he touched. He turned on the shower and pulled off his shorts. "Oh, Jeez, what a mess," he said as he stepped in. "Holy Christ, what a mess." The walls of the shower ran red.

While Kyle was still at the clinic, Glen McNichol ran to the other end of Gold River's government campus, his long knife still in hand, and found Royal Canadian Mounted Police constable Rick McKerracher. The two went to the stairs and almost immediately spotted a cougar. It crouched and bared its teeth. McKerracher killed it with a shot to the head. They carried the carcass to the RCMP office, where McKerracher posed with it for newspaper photos that flashed across Canada the next day.

John hurriedly packed a bag, but he'd need cash, he muttered. He had no cash.

"Don't leave, Dad," Brad said. "Hang on a minute."

Puffing back up the stairs from his basement bedroom, Brad handed John a small wad of bills. John hadn't cried when he found Kyle face down and motionless. He'd kept his cool at the clinic and as he'd watched the helicopter take his boy away. But now, holding Brad's savings, he felt the tears come. It felt good to have someone take care of him. He pulled Brad close and held on. Kyle had looked like hell, but he had asked a question and answered one. He was going to make it.

At the hospital in Campbell River, John was ushered into a

cold operating room full of instruments and rolling dollies. Two staffers huddled off to one side. Kyle lay motionless under a gauze drape with the operating light beating down on him. His Tazmanian Devil underwear were lying in the trash. John stopped short. There was no one tending the boy.

He didn't breathe again until someone explained that Kyle was alive, but needed the skills of big city surgeons. John had seen that torn little face and realized they were right. They were flying Kyle to Children's Hospital in Vancouver. John held his hand and talked to him, telling him to just think about breathing. The little white fingers pressed back, light against John's hard palm.

Joan arrived in time to fly to Vancouver with John. They reached Children's Hospital around 1:00 P.M. At 3:00 P.M., the surgery began. Hospital staff told John and Joan to go get settled at the Easter Seals house for parents of young patients. The operation was expected to last fourteen hours.

They were back at the hospital by 4:00 A.M. At about 7:00 A.M., the plastic surgeon came to the private room where they waited. Doctor Nancy Van Laeken pulled off her surgical cap and sat in a heavy upholstered chair next to John and Joan. Tall, slim, and handsome, she was still in surgical booties and scrubs. She looked tired.

"I can't believe he's alive," she told them. But they needed to forget any hopes that they'd see Kyle's old face again. The doctor said she had several pieces of his cheekbone on ice. Some of those pieces might be refitted in later surgeries. She spelled out the options for face and scalp reconstruction and walked them through the process of installing a glass eye.

"You're very lucky to still have him," she said.

This was much worse than John had expected. Kyle had spoken, answered questions. Didn't that mean he'd be fine? He tried to pay attention. Now Dr. Van Laeken was describing the wires that were holding Kyle's face together. Shock, the body shutting down organs in response to blood loss and dehydration, was the next threat, another doctor who joined them said. The doctors also warned that animal bites can cause lethal infections. John stiffened at the realization that Kyle was still in danger, not just in need of patching up.

Finally they called John and Joan to see their boy. "He looks so good," said a smiling nurse who stopped them along the way.

John looked anxiously around. The last time he had been in a big hospital, Kyle was a premature baby in the tidy, cheerful neonatal care unit. This wide-open intensive care ward looked like a war zone. The pace was quick. It was crowded with whispering doctors and nurses hovering over motionless patients buried in gear. This wasn't a broken-bone and stitches ward, it was a heart attack, bleed-to-death, burned-to-death ward.

John and Joan slowed when they reached Kyle's bed. The puffy face lay on a white pillow. Countless stitches pulled against the swelling, purple flesh. When Joan saw Kyle's face, she turned back to John, hand on her mouth. He realized she hadn't had any idea what the cougar had done. Kyle had already been wrapped in gauze when she got to Campbell River. He could feel his strong wife struggle and then give in to her tears, shaking and sobbing against his chest.

But John was smiling. Kyle was plugged into beeping machines like everyone else in the room. He had tubes in his throat and feet, and stitches all over. But John had seen worse when he rolled Kyle over in the bush. Through all the stitches and swelling bruises, he could see his son again. "Oh my God," he thought, realizing he'd been right all along. "He's going to be OK."

6

The Cougar Stairs

Gold River, B.C., a milltown bulldozed into the forest in 1965, is home to frequent cougar sightings.

Viewed from the air, the Gold River Valley seems all forest and fjord. Most of Vancouver Island's people live on the other side of the island. The Gold River side looks like a temperate jungle, often misty with remnants of rain and the exhalations of millions of conifers. Clear-cut scars mark almost every mountain, but mostly the senses are struck by riotous growth from underbrush to overstory.

The town of Gold River didn't grow naturally. It was built all at once in 1965 to the specifications of the Tahsis Paper Company, which was installing a huge new pulp mill on the nearby river delta. The company needed about two thousand people, loggers and the engineers, technicians, and laborers to run the mill. Laid out in neat grids with a pedestrian shopping mall at its center, Gold River thirty years later looked like a movie set on which the paint was still drying. If it sounds idyllic, it was. Until the youngest Musselman boy was nearly killed by a cougar on his way to school.

What Gold River had forgotten is that here, the line between town and bush is about as meaningful as the stripes of a painted cattle guard. Streets, streetlights, and sidewalks mark the edge of town for humans, but bears and cougars don't care. They forage among Gold River houses as they do in the forest across the road.

Months after the attack, Gold River was still trying to recover. But on the sunny day when Kyle came home, the town confronted another painful lesson: some events leave a person, or a town, forever changed. There is no easy security among predators once you believe they can hurt you.

A kid-painted welcome poster hung over the city limits sign where a police escort waited. The clapping and cheering began before John and Joan's van turned onto Donner Street. Balloons and streamers lashed in the breeze and the bright shiny sound of children's voices filled the street. People were ready to be reassured at the sight of the boy recovered, ready to put the horror behind them.

Riding high in the front seat of his parent's van, Kyle waved to the clapping and cheering crowd of schoolchildren, teachers, and neighbors. He spotted his best friend Johnny Watts, who'd sent tape-recorded letters to the hospital. Kyle swung the van door open and stepped down.

Johnny's mother, Denise, started to shake. Before, Kyle had been a little chubby. Now he was emaciated. Only one side of his face moved as he bravely smiled into the ring of staring eyes. Bright pink scars traced the path of claws through his eye and forehead. His nose was off-center and his right eyelid drooped over a dark implant. He wore a bandana on his head, but it couldn't hide the fact that he had little or no hair left. All Denise could see was a small tuft below his ears. It all looked so painful.

Johnny, who had been dancing with excitement, froze. Kyle walked to him through the crowd. "Hi, John" he said.

Johnny turned and ran. Denise caught up with him on the highway. "That's not Kyle," Johnny wailed. "It's got his voice, but it's not his face."

Kyle not only looked different, he had lost the verve that had made him a favorite around town. He jumped anytime someone crushed a sheet of paper or rattled a plastic food wrapper. It sounded like the cougar moving in the brush, he said.

Gold River didn't look different at all, but it too was changing. Gone was the naïve assurance that a town could, by appearing tidy, secure, and rational, exempt itself from the bush and the dangers that might wander from it. The little town wasn't near the bush, it was enveloped by it, a tiny human encampment surrounded by a wilder world.

Now what? How could townspeople feel secure again? A few obvious steps immediately presented themselves.

The morning of the attack, Dale Frame walked down to the staircase from his house in Scout Lake Subdivision. There he found Glen McNichol, whom he knew from the mill. Glen had an idea. They had to cut the alder thicket back. Otherwise, another cat could lie three feet from the edge of the path, as Kyle's attacker had, and not be seen until it was again too late. By noon, he and Glen had parked their pickups at the top of the stairs and unloaded chainsaws. Dale yanked the starter cord and set to work. They felled trees downhill, cutting a 20-foot swath on both sides of the stairs.

His saw wailed and threw bone-white dust. Dale had moved to Gold River when it was little more than a bulldozed clear-cut at the end of the highway. The cougars had always been around, but as the trees grew back, the deer came, too, bringing the cougars closer. You couldn't blame the cougar, Frame planned to remind people. It had been a young and hungry cat presented with an easy meal and perfect ambush cover.

That cover was vanishing fast. Within an hour, Dale and Glen had attracted volunteers. Every once in a while, he'd straighten his back and look around. Axe-wielding mothers were hacking off low branches at the clearing's edge. People looked serious and worried as reports came in from the hospital. Critical condition, they heard. Respirators. Surgery.

The staircase looked good with a haircut. For the first time in years, you could stand at the top and see all the way down to the bottom.

Parents met later the same week with Pat Brown-Clayton, Jerry Brunham, and Knut Atkinson from the Ministry of Environment. A little boy had almost been killed. They wanted to know what the ministry would do to prevent another attack.

There would be no wholesale cougar hunt, Gold River residents were told, and nothing short of that would make much difference. Scout Lake Subdivision overlaid the ancient migration trails of game animals, Brown-Clayton said. Having built your town in a river bottom in the bush, you'd have to expect wild animals to pass through and occasionally do unpredictable things. Attacks are awful, the game wardens agreed, but you can't kill off all the cougars because of one freak event. The Ministry of Environment's job is to protect wildlife, not wipe it out.

None of that was comforting if you'd seen John Musselman running across the highway with a bloody bundle in his arms. A line of cars began showing up at the schoolyard every morning and afternoon. People who had chosen Gold River as a place to raise their kids away from busy traffic and dangerous strangers were now driving their kids to school, just as they would have in the big cities they had fled.

But that only protected your fifth-grader until she hopped from the car. Some residents needed more. They kicked around a plan to fire up a siren any time a cougar was sighted. They looked for cougar repellant to spread around town and talked about

*Gold River children began calling this staircase "the cougar stairs," after
Kyle Musselman was attacked on them as he walked to school in 1994.
Parents still supervise their children on the stairs.*

building a fence down both sides of what kids were now calling
the Cougar Stairs. But no one saw Kyle's cougar before it struck,
so a siren wouldn't have helped. There is no such thing as a permanent cougar repellant and the fences would just force
migrating bears and cougars up into Scout Lake Subdivision or
down into the schoolyard.

John Musselman came home to Gold River angry. He'd grown
up in a logging family on the mainland, where cougar sightings

were rare. But these animals around Gold River were not afraid of people, John told reporters. There were weeks in which a cougar was sighted in town every day, he told them. People were so scared they wouldn't let their kids play outside or walk three blocks to the store, John said. Less than a week after they'd brought Kyle home, John and Joan were out for an evening walk when their dog started barking. John walked over to investigate and found himself face to face with another cougar. Clearly there were too many cougars. Every cougar that came to town should be shot.

At that time, John still suffered screaming nightmares of the bloody hash of Kyle's head. But day by day, as he watched Kyle go to school without hiding his scars and muster the courage to ride his bike and play hockey one-eyed, John too felt stronger.

The nightmares faded. His anger cooled. He drove the kids to school when he could and forbade them to take the staircase shortcut when he couldn't. But he also began saying "You can't kill everything off just because you're afraid of them and there's been an accident. It's one of them things in life...You know, it happens."

Bonnie Bellwood, another Scout Lake resident, accepted the slim risk, too. Four years after Kyle's attack, her older kids were some of the few who still walked to school alone and played in the bush as kids had done for thirty years in Gold River.

September 4, 1998, dawned unusually sunny and warm for a fall day on the north end of Vancouver Island. In her house at 420 Donner Street, Bonnie roused her twelve-year-old son, Brandon, her nine-year-old daughter, Britney, and her kindergartner, Chelsea. Awake and finally moving, Chelsea dressed in black lace-up boots, black leggings, and a pink fleece sweatshirt. Breakfast was toast and peanut butter served by her mum, who gently bossed the kids along. As usual, Britney left first with a friend. Brandon left when he wouldn't have to be seen with Britney. Then Chelsea slung up her pink and white cartoon backpack, grabbed her mother's hand, and headed out the door. The 100-foot staircase that connects the subdivision to the schoolyard was just two doors up the street.

Wearing a pink housecoat and flip-flops, Bonnie stopped at the top of the stairs and kissed Chelsea goodbye. "Watch crossing the road and go right to your class," she said as the little girl trudged down the stairs. "Bye mom," Chelsea said. She took a few steps and turned around, "See ya later, mom."

Chelsea was nearly at the bottom when Bonnie first saw the bear. Big and black, it stepped onto the paved path beside her. Chelsea looked tiny as she spun around to look for her mom. It seemed like even at that distance Bonnie could see her daughter's wide eyes through her glasses.

Bonnie couldn't make a sound. She ran four steps toward her child then stopped, afraid to aggravate the bear. She backed up to the top and hated that, too. She imagined herself yelling, "Chelsea, come here now!" but that didn't seem right, either.

As she'd been taught in cougar safety lessons, Chelsea hollered and put her hands above her head. Then she crouched down as if to hide.

The bear looked at the little girl but kept walking. It pooped out two eight-inch-long scats purple with fall berries. They steamed on the blacktop as the bear shambled out of the logged zone and into the forest. Bonnie ran down and Chelsea scrambled into her arms.

"I was playing invisible," she said as they climbed back to the street at the top.

They waited there for a minute and then walked to school together. Bonnie thought about her decision to let her children walk the Cougar Stairs and run in the woods. There were parents who wouldn't let their kids play at her house because of it. But she knew that Kyle's attack, four years before, had been a fluke. Chelsea's encounter just now was a fluke. Bonnie's kids were as safe today as they'd been all the years they'd been running carefree about town.

Nevertheless, at noon, she drove down and picked Chelsea up for lunch. The school had been rebuilt since Kyle's attack, but the same queue of parents lined up at the new building's front doors as had appeared there the day he was mauled.

"I could have petted him, mum," the little girl said.

"No joke, Chels. You could have rode him."

Bonnie picked Chelsea up again at the end of the day.

7
Hunting the Truth

Hornocker Wildlife Institute biologist Scott Relyea had to be lowered over the lip of a cliff to retrieve this drugged subject, captured in Montana's Paradise Valley outside Yellowstone National Park.

The young cougar had recently fought for and won his 75-square-mile territory in New Mexico's San Andres Mountains. Now, ears and lips tacked back in a futile snarl, left front leg caught in a loop of cabled steel, he stared at his captors through narrowed amber eyes.

Biologist Linda Sweanor was not afraid of the big predator crouched before her. Experience had taught her that the typical cougar would vastly prefer to run than confront a human. But this cat couldn't run, so the research team stayed cautiously out of range until the tranquilizing dart found the animal's muscular haunch. The drug worked fast. Within a few moments, Linda crouched over a semi-conscious cat. His eyes were still open, but he seemed glassily blind to the presence of humans. Knocking him out completely would be safer for the researchers but riskier for the cat. A heavily drugged animal can't, for instance, maintain body temperature on a cold day. And a groggy, slow-to-recover cat is an easy target for predators, including other cougars.

The team worked efficiently, slipping the snare from the heavy leg, measuring and weighing. He was beautifully fit and, at 145 pounds, large for his kind. They tattooed an identifying mark in one ear, clipped a plastic tag to the other, and encircled his neck with a battery-operated radio collar weighing 1 pound. The collar made his neat, round head appear even smaller, incongruous on the big body stretched before them. Their receivers would be able to hear the collar's signal miles away. Linda was pleased to note the toe, once broken, which jutted from his right forefoot: it would give him a signature track.

Wildlife researchers try not to get sentimental about their subjects, so they labeled more than named him. Since he was the third Linda Sweanor and her colleagues had snared, he would be called Male 3.

The year was 1985. Linda and her husband Kenny Logan were beginning the most intensive long-term cougar study ever attempted, under the auspices of a nonprofit predator research group called the Hornocker Wildlife Institute. The project would run year-round for a decade, eventually involving eight researchers and 294 cougars scattered across time and the San Andres Mountains, a rugged and remote 80-mile-long range in the Chihuahuan Desert. Linda would follow Male 3's signal and broken-toed track, in small planes and on foot, for nine of those ten years.

Why all this effort? Because that's what it takes to peek into the secret world of the cougar.

Even with the help of radio collars, though, all researchers get is a distant view, a chance to map the movements of individual cougars over the phases of their lives. When a typical cougar researcher actually sees her elusive subject, it's usually because the animal is dead or being captured. Even a massive effort like Linda's can't tell researchers how wild cougar kittens play or what the probably tense encounters between solitary adults look like. Do cougar mothers teach kittens how to hunt? Do families hunt cooperatively? Nobody knows, because nobody gets to watch.

There are lucky exceptions, like the time Montanan Tom Parker found a dead white-tailed deer near a vacation cabin down the road from his house. Tom is a professional tracker who works with cougar researchers, so he knew it was a cougar kill, and a recent one. He contacted a friend who owned a fancy video camera. The two set it up and left. The tape shows an adult female and two or possibly three kittens visiting the kill one at a time. Each comes in silently, feeds for a few minutes, then steps away and chirps like a bird. After one leaves, another silently appears and begins to feed, only to get up in a little while, chirp and leave. Is this a typical wild cougar feeding scene? Nobody knows.

Despite their limitations, radio collar studies are the best tool researchers have to unlock the secrets of the cougar. They work like this: researchers like Sweanor and Logan select an area they will study, say a mountain range or a national park. Within that area they may try to collar every cougar or, depending on funding and what they want to learn, just a few. Then, for months or years, the collared cats are located regularly by their unique radio signals. They might be located once a week to find out how large their territories are; or every fifteen minutes for twenty four hours, to see how far they travel, when they rest, or how long it takes them to finish eating a deer.

Collar signals are nothing more than staticky beeps of varying speed and intensity, so even a collared cat isn't easy to find. Signals are most easily picked up from a small plane but most accurately pinpointed on foot by time-consuming triangulation. In rugged country, these signals can bounce about like kids' shouted echoes, sending a researcher trudging farther and farther up a mountain's flank when her subject is hiding in a thicket below.

By comparison, the work of getting the collars on must seem easy. Two key tools are required: well-trained hounds and an experienced houndsman. Once fresh tracks are found—by far, the most time-consuming part of cat hunting—the handler releases one or more hounds upon the scent. Cougars seldom run far when chased by baying hounds. The dogs follow the scent trail until they reach the tree up which the cougar has fled. There they leap, paw, and bark, effectively holding the cat until the handler arrives. The fact that nearly all cougars tree when chased by hounds makes capture relatively safe for researchers, their dogs, and unwilling subjects alike.

In the nearly treeless desert of Linda Sweanor's New Mexico study, however, cougars could only run. The big cats are lightning-quick but lack endurance, so dogs would have caught the cats on the ground, a recipe for bloodshed on both sides. A solution came from woodsman and trapper Frank Smith, who had killed perhaps three hundred cats for sport or as part of his job as a New Mexico depredation control officer. Smith taught the Hornocker researchers about leghold snares.

Trappers lure other species with food, but cougars aren't easily baited: they prefer to kill their own meals. Smith taught placement, how a cougar trapper must study the animal's movements, then hide snares along its favorite routes. The researchers learned how to position rocks or other obstacles around a hidden snare to lead the animal's foot onto the spring-loaded trip plate.

The technique worked. The team eventually radio-collared 107 cougars, including broken-toed Male 3. At any one time, the resident population of the study area was thirty adults and fifteen to thirty kittens, spread thin: less than five animals per 100 square miles. Kittens collared young were recollared as they grew larger. Adults were captured and recollared every few years as batteries wore down or equipment failed.

But successful wildlife researchers are nothing if not patient. Since the 1960s, when a young Ph.D. candidate named Maurice

Photo by Bob Wiesner

This cougar was captured in Montana's Garnet Range, ear-tagged for identification, and radio-collared. The moment of capture may be the only time some researchers see cougars, which are otherwise just beeps on a radio tracking device.

Hornocker undertook the first intensive radio collar cougar study, biologists like Linda have accumulated a surprising amount of information about what is probably the continent's most secretive predator.

For instance, researchers know the answer to this question: Are there really more cougars in the woods these days?

The answer is yes. Absolutely. Taken as a species, cougars are not rare or endangered by a long shot. They were, perhaps, once. Bounty hunted as vermin until the late 1950s, cougars were almost completely eradicated in the East and their range severely limited in the West, until they could be found only in rugged, remote country.

But public attitudes changed, the bounties came off, and one by one western states began to protect cougars. Finally, all but Texas offered at least the protection of hunting quotas. More important, deer herds recovered from intensive, turn-of-the-century market hunting that had nearly wiped them out in many regions. Where they were too few to recover, deer were reintroduced.

Photo by Bob Wiesner

Even the largest cougar usually trees when startled or chased by hounds.

Soon a plentiful cougar food supply again roamed the continent, and the cougar again flourished.

More recently, California voters banned recreational cougar hunting outright, apparently agreeing with the referendum's sponsors that hound hunting is cruel and pointless, but also partly because of a persistent belief that the species is still at risk. Then Washington and Oregon banned hound hunting. Without hounds to locate and tree cats, hunter success rates in those states dropped. Unhunted cougar populations with room to expand can grow up to 28 percent a year, rapidly recolonizing suitable habitat for hundreds of miles in every direction.

Another thing researchers have learned is that cougars, if unhunted, do *not* continue to multiply until they overpopulate their range. Hunting as a population control is only necessary if the goal is to keep cougar numbers artificially low. Linda Sweanor and her colleagues watched it happen in New Mexico. As their study cats reached carrying capacity, growth slowed to almost zero. Cougar numbers are still increasing in some parts of the West, but that's because they existed at bounty-enforced lows for generations,

Research houndsman Bob Wiesner's English bluetick hound barking under a treed cougar.

and they haven't yet reached biological carrying capacity.

Political carrying capacity is, of course, another matter. It may be that cougars have already exceeded this limit across most of their western range, which is why cougar quotas have been raised in states like Montana, Utah, and Idaho, and Washington legislators have demanded a return to hound hunting.

But game managers would be hard-pressed to devise population controls as efficient as those of the cats themselves. For instance, it is probably common for females to abandon kittens they cannot provide for because of game scarcity or infirmity. In Arizona, researcher Harley Shaw observed a female with three eight-week-old kittens who, after being captured and tranquilized twice in a few days, fled the second capture site without them. She never returned.

Some ten days later, the kittens died near where they had been left clinging to three small trees. Two weeks after that, the female was found curled beneath a juniper as though asleep. Like her kittens, she had apparently starved to death.

Young cougars are abandoned by their mothers after eighteen months to two years or more in her care. Presumably confused, perhaps afraid, they may wait weeks for her return. But eventually the young cats begin to search for a home range of their own. Some females and nearly all males travel so far that they leave the population into which they were born. Only the smartest and most cautious survive this rite of passage.

And at any age, a cougar—male, female, or kitten—who encounters a big territorial male may be killed. As populations increase, so do encounters between cats and, presumably, intraspecies killings.

A widely held myth is that cats, if not heavily hunted, will eat all the deer. Many people who say there are "too many" cougars are hunters afraid that cougars are killing too many deer. One reason cougars were bountied in the first place was their taste for deer flesh. Researchers estimate that adult cougars, given the opportunity, kill one deer or other large ungulate every seven to fourteen or more days. That can sound like a lot of killing.

It is also true that cougars will kill more than they need, particularly when prey can't escape—penned sheep, for instance. Called surplus killing, this apparent wastefulness is partly how cougars earned their centuries-old reputation for wanton destruction. One current myth about cougars, a modern attempt to revise the cougar into a kinder, gentler predator, is that surplus killing doesn't actually happen, that it's an old, Wild West story. Not so. A single cougar can easily kill dozens of domestic sheep in a night, or several deer within a few hundred yards of each other.

Along similar lines, you often hear that cougars and other predators kill the old and weak. They improve a herd's health the way a careful gardener prunes to strengthen his trees. Not so. Studies have found that cougars like to kill vulnerable fawns. They also kill a significant percentage of big bucks, probably because bucks are more frequently alone and are distracted and therefore vulnerable during the fall rut.

But despite their zest for killing and their willingness to take prime animals, researchers have learned that under normal circumstances cougars do not limit deer herds. There aren't enough cougars. There aren't supposed to be: the two species evolved side by side, cougars spread thin and deer in teeming herds. What limits deer herds are more pervasive events like heavy winter snows, poor forage during a drought, or habitat lost to human development or poorly planned logging. However, those who study the critically endangered bighorn sheep in California testify that one cougar with a taste for sheep flesh *can* have a dramatic impact on a population already beleaguered by disease and habitat loss.

Beware of the numbers bandied by those who argue the over- or underpopulation of cougars. The truth is, nobody can say how many cougars wander the woods, because biologists can't simply drive into the hills and count, as they do with deer and nesting waterfowl. They can count cougar tracks. They can count hunter-killed and road-killed cougars. They can guess how many cougars live in one area based on a known number of cougars in a radio collar study area. But these techniques only alert game managers to changes.

So when a newspaper reports that 2,500 cougars live in Washington State, remember that that's shorthand for "Researchers' best guess, based on years of best guesses, is that 2,500 cougars, give or take, live in Washington." Some states, like Idaho and Montana, won't even venture an official guess. California's estimate of 5,100 animals was calculated back in 1988 and is still considered by some as good a number as any, although others have revised the guess to 6,000.

A subtle misconception, implied in all discussions of "the cougar," including this book, deserves mention. It's dangerous to overgeneralize, to talk too much about "the cougar," as though all were the same. Mountain lions are extremely adaptable and highly individual. Once they lived in most of the continent's ecosystems, from desert canyonlands to scrub oak hills to alpine forest, from east coast to west. Individual cougar populations are unique enough in behavior, diet, and average size that experts still argue about how many subspecies there are.

For example, scientists have learned that the farther north you travel, the bigger the average cougar. In some places, cougars often kill each other. In others, they don't. Some seem more willing to behave aggressively toward humans. Cougars in Arizona–and *no place else*–regularly kill cattle. In that state, a typical cougar might eat more beef than venison. Cats elsewhere have the opportunity to kill cattle, but they mostly refrain. Some cougars engage in surplus killing. Others don't. Most tree when chased by baying hounds. A few don't. Most strongly prefer deer when deer are available. A few mow through precious remnant herds of bighorn sheep. All this behavioral and perhaps genetic variation means that it's risky, albeit sometimes necessary, to generalize about "the cougar" based on a few observations, a hundred interviews, or even a careful radio collar study.

Equally risky are simple responses to the escalation of cougar incidents and attacks. Researchers speculate warily about possible solutions, but they are sure of little except this: The disgusted game manager who said, "If we want fewer attacks, we need to shoot more cougars," was wrong, even though this is the course of action that Montana, for instance, has embraced. Researchers see evidence that human actions contribute to the increase in attacks, so how likely is more human interference to eliminate it, short of wiping out the species?

Our impacts are both direct and indirect. As humans bulldoze and build cougars into smaller and smaller chunks of usable habitat, it must set off seismic shocks in a social dynamic designed to spread cougars thinly across huge areas. When hunters kill up to a fourth of a region's adult cougar population annually, what happens to the cats' carefully balanced hierarchy? How long could a human culture withstand a death rate that high or that unnaturally skewed? In unhunted cougar populations, the highest death rates are among the young, and cougars who reach adulthood generally survive to reproduce. In hunted populations, the opposite is true: adults die rapidly. One idea, called the Big Tom Theory, says that when a big territorial male is killed, several subadults who would normally have died or emigrated divide the dead cat's territory, increasing the number of cats that can live in that area. This is important because young animals seem to initiate a disproportionate number of cougar attacks. So standard hunting practices may be skewing cougar populations toward the very individuals least unlikely to avoid humans.

Our impacts may be genetic as well as social. Hunters, for instance, prefer to take big males. Big males are the successful animals that would ordinarily pass along their successful genes. It may be that successful cougars tend to be cautious animals, unlikely to confront humans and therefore quick to tree and easy to kill. One trait remaining to the survivors who ran or fought instead of treeing might be foolhardiness.

On the other hand, California has not allowed sport hunting since 1971. There, generations of cougars have lived free of hunting pressure except for those killed on problem cougar permits. You might expect California to be a fairly peaceful place, as far as cougars go. It's not. The state has recorded more attacks than any cougar region except British Columbia. Hunting advocates point to California as proof that cougars must be extensively hunted to keep people safe. But the area with more cougar problems than California is Vancouver Island. Vancouver Island has hunted its cougars intensively since settlement. Besides, California cougars *are* hunted. Nearly as many are taken on depredation permits today as were, in some pre-ban years, taken by recreational hunters.

To appreciate the end of Male 3's story, you have to know this: cougars' lives are incredibly precarious. Older cougars show their years in blunted canines, worn incisors, healed scars, and notched ears. A cougar with sharp white teeth and no scars is a young cat. Or a zoo animal. An old cougar is lucky, smart, or more likely both.

Lives are shortened by hunters and, in populated areas, by cars. One hunted population of cougars in Wyoming had, as its oldest adult, a seven-year-old (cougars in captivity live twenty years or more). An early 1980s cougar study returned few useful results because most of the animals were killed by hunters within a few months after collaring. Maurice Hornocker's first study site was moved after nearly all fourteen of his first winter's study cougars were shot before the snow melted in the spring.

New Mexico's San Andres Mountains are almost completely roadless and not heavily hunted. Yet the San Andres cats Linda Sweanor and her husband followed did not live twenty years, either. What killed them? In most cases, it wasn't their arduous lives as lone hunters, or disease, or injuries incurred in botched attempts to kill big ungulates. The primary cause of death in the San Andres was adult male cougars.

Other predators also kill cougars. Bob Wiesner, houndsman and tracker for Hornocker researcher Kerry Murphy, once hiked deep into Yellowstone country to find a collared female who hadn't moved in days. The houndsman followed the signal to a rocky bluff. He found coyote tracks pocking the drifted snow around a deep, vertical crack. Closer examination of the crack revealed a sad sight a few yards below: the cat's tightly wedged body. Rubbed-off hair and hide told the probable tale: she had fled the coyotes by diving into the only refuge she could find, only to be trapped and slowly killed by it.

Male 3 stands out in Linda Sweanor's mind years after her study ended for one simple reason. He did what only very smart, very lucky cougars do: he survived. Male 3 was recaptured four times during the New Mexico study for recollaring; otherwise his life was uneventful, a luxury among lions. He was middle-aged when Frank and the scientists set out to snare him one more time.

This time, the capture wasn't about battery replacement. The researchers wanted to study forced relocation as a management tool. Relocation has been used for decades to separate bears from the problems they cause, with much public support but a crashing lack of success. The joke is that the bear beats the ranger home, since the ranger must obey speed limits. Was the technique as ineffective for cougars? To find out, the Hornocker researchers began removing cougars from one section of their study area. Male 3 was among those slated for relocation.

The researchers tried to trap him for six months. They set snares along his travel routes. He stepped around them. Their trapper, Frank, suggested they set two snares, one obvious and one hidden, so that a cat dealing with the first would step in the second. Male 3 sprang both.

One day, while setting snares near a kill surrounded by Male 3's big, jut-toed tracks, Linda looked up to see the patriarch himself staring at her. A frozen second passed; then he turned, tail-tip twitching, and glided away. When she was sure he was gone, she laid her snares.

Linda returned the next day to find she had finally won: Male 3 was caught. Then she realized that the cougar spitting and snarling at her was too small. It was a young male who'd snuck in to examine the kill. It's impossible to know what Male 3 made of this series of events, but the big cat abruptly stopped returning to his kills.

The researchers finally gave up; they had removed thirteen animals from the test area. Male 3 remained. They monitored his movements, exasperated and a little admiring, as he took advantage of the unintended gift, expanding his territory until it encompassed all the vacated ones.

Meanwhile, Linda and the other researchers confirmed what they already knew: capture and relocation is not just ineffective, it's often fatal. Relocated cougars do have a chance, but it's slim, slimmest of all for mature territorial adults who have spent their lives learning how to hunt and stay safe in their territories. Most relocated cats die trying to return home—or they fail to hunt successfully in their strange surroundings; they meet up with an aggressive territorial male; or they get in trouble with pets or livestock.

A sad story comes from the Kalispell, Montana area, where in 1997 a female and nearly grown kitten were relocated after attacking a dog in Glacier National Park. At capture, the female weighed 120 pounds. A month later the female, now alone, killed a cocker spaniel and dragged it under a trailer in the little town of Essex. She was shot by wildlife officers. In those four weeks, she had lost a third of her body weight: at death, she weighed only 80 pounds.

When a collared cougar is immobile for six hours, a mercury switch in his collar trips, and the transmission changes. Researchers call it a mortality signal. One day in 1994, Linda picked up a mortality signal on Male 3. Saddened, she hiked toward the source. The researchers were nearly at their project's conclusion. It would have been nice to pack up the camps and radio gear, the data charts and maps, knowing the wily old cougar was still out there.

But the signal had been accurate: Male 3 was dead. Examining the big cat made Linda feel better, though. He was perhaps thirteen, luxuriously old for a wild cougar. There was fur in his mouth, and mule deer liver and kidney filled his belly. His fresh kill sprawled before him. He had died, full of fire and a fine meal, simply of old age. Of 294 cougars Linda and her colleagues studied those ten years, only four were tough enough and smart enough to earn a peaceful death.

8
The Urban Cougar

Washington Department of Fish and Wildlife Sgt. Ray Kahler overlooking downtown Spokane, Washington, where he has captured bear and moose and chased cougar.

The radio in Ray Kahler's truck crackles: "P.D. reports a young moose sighted at Ferris, last seen headed east."

Ray keys his mike to tell the dispatcher he's on his way and wheels his truck around. He's a Washington Department of Fish and Wildlife game warden, and sometimes hunting nuisance wildlife is his job. But Ray isn't headquartered in mountainous backcountry. He will hunt this moose in midday traffic in Spokane, Washington, a city of 400,000. Ferris is one of the biggest high schools in town.

Miles south, city streets give way to a checkerboard of hilly wheat fields and timber: Washington's Palouse region. The moose likely came from there, Ray says, working its way along creekbeds, across hobby farms, and then from yard to yard until it found itself in the cheek-by-jowl neighborhood around Ferris. Happens all the time, he says.

Ray prowls a dirt lane through some vacant lots between Ferris and a gated subdivision, easing to a stop every few feet to peer into bushes and pasture grass. Nothing. One careful loop of the school grounds and he radios in to report no luck. A moose, unmistakable and huge even in adolescence, has appeared and disappeared in the middle of the city. It will probably escape town without incident, Kahler predicts. Most of them do, and that's good. Capture and removal is dangerous for human and moose alike.

Tall, muscular, and marked by the sun, Ray looks the part of a professional outdoorsman. Standing on a rocky bluff on Spokane's South Hill, he points to the row of high-rise office towers downtown and tells how a bear foraged its way up the banks of the Spokane River until it was discovered in Riverside Park, smack in the middle of the buildings. Ray captured it just blocks from the boutiques and department stores that face the Opera House.

He peers over the cliff edge into the asphalt canyons between St. Luke's, Sacred Heart, Deaconess, and Shriner's hospitals. A cougar got away from him there. It was killing cats and dogs in the yards of the neighborhood's few remaining private homes. Ray scoured alleys every time he got a report, but the cat moved along before he could capture it.

In nearly every western city, there's a Ray Kahler who is now learning to track big game down city streets. Just as residents of tiny mountain towns like Gold River, British Columbia learned, western urbanites are discovering that while leafy backyards and parks aren't great wildlife habitat, they'll do. Especially when those backyards were once wildlands.

Urban wildlife is nothing new. Squirrels and birds have long been welcomed at window feeders. Deer are tolerated as attractive nuisances. Urbanites may eventually accept the bear that strips fruit trees or knocks over garbage cans. Even easier to accept is the moose living off the third fairway, browsing water plants. A cougar that, on that same golf course, kills and eats deer probably will not be accepted. And yet the cougar may be better suited to life in our cities than moose or bear. The fairway moose would not long escape detection, but the cougar would, at least until he chose the wrong prey, say, a pet. Urban cougar tales illustrate how well cougars have adapted to people. They also raise the question whether people will ever adapt to sharing their cities with cougars.

In Boulder, Colorado, researchers Jim Halfpenny and Michael Sanders learned that by the mid-1980s there were dozens of cougars hunting the city at least part-time. They asked citizens to call with sightings. One caller had watched a cougar give birth under a neighbor's porch. Another watched a cougar scale a roof to bat at a weathervane. Workers at Boulder Community Hospital spied one lounging on an outdoor deck at the medical center, while other callers described a cougar that fed on a deer carcass as a crowd of sixty people watched. One Boulder elementary school's sandbox was found to be serving double duty: playground equipment by day, cougar litter box by night.

Halfpenny was once summoned from bed by a swing-dancing enthusiast who spotted a cougar as he left a downtown bar. Halfpenny's renown as a tracker takes him to remote corners of the world, but that late-night expedition, conducted by the light of streetlamps, took him down the middle of a business-district street.

In Salt Lake City, game warden Bill Bates has become an expert at the downtown cougar hunt. He knows just how to crawl up onto the hood of a shiny new Chevy Suburban to dart a cat hiding in a garage. Another time, he darted a cougar in a basement window well. A third cougar, a youngster, was discovered hiding under a large squash plant when the homeowner walked out his back door to pick some vegetables for dinner.

In April of 1998, dogs and cats started disappearing from a

neighborhood near city hall in Olympia, Washington. The mystery was solved when residents spotted a cougar in the brushy ravine behind their homes. It rushed a wildlife officer and was shot.

A cougar in Gresham, Oregon, a suburb of Portland, walked right into an elementary school. A teacher found it in the foyer. The animal dashed out of the building, spooked a janitor in the parking lot, and then climbed a nearby board fence before treeing in a backyard.

The cougar that police officer Lori Kratzer spotted on the campus of Stanford University slipped away before it could be caught. Officials say the dozens of cougars seen every year in Bay Area suburbs mostly do the same. The landscape is brushy and the cats are quick.

In Sacramento, wildlife capture expert Bob Teagle can look out the window of California Department of Fish and Game's downtown headquarters onto a riverside greenbelt, where he occasionally finds cougar tracks. He believes the prints belong not to wandering cats, but to resident cougars who have learned to hunt deer and other wildlife along the American River as it sweeps through town. As long as they're not bothering anyone, he's decided not to bother them.

How do big, wary predators wind up in bright, noisy cities? The same way Ray Kahler's moose made it into Spokane and then vanished without a trace. We all but invite them.

For cougars, the invitation began with suburban sprawl. For most of the 1990s, census data shows that more Americans moved to suburbs than to cities. New suburban neighborhoods gobble land fast, which is partly why Seattle's acreage grew more than twice as fast as its population from 1970 to 1990, and Los Angeles sprawled six times faster than it added people.

In those same years, cougar populations were growing, too. As their density increased, the search for unclaimed territory forced successive generations of cougars farther from the remote strongholds to which the animals retreated in the bounty era, closer and closer to humans.

Where Cougars Strike

Fifty-three cougar attacks occurred in North America during the last decade. Almost none happened in remote wilderness, where people might expect to be at risk.

Urban areas	0
Within sight of human dwellings	7
Developed campsites or campgrounds	6
Trails or roads	24
Remote backcountry	1
Unknown	*15

Some reports compiled by wildlife agencies do not provide complete descriptions of attack locales.

Source: Authors' survey of attack reports 1990-1999.

The state of Montana has hired a "problem wildlife officer" for the area around the resort town of Kalispell. Eric Wenum fields up to sixty cougar calls a month in the summer, his busy season. Soon after his job was created in 1994, he was summoned to a well-tended neighborhood three blocks east of Kalispell's city hall. A cougar had killed a house cat there and had lain down on a manicured lawn to eat it.

A 100-plus-pound wild animal doesn't stroll through a busy town clear to its grassy, tree-shaded heart and find a meal. Here's how it happens. Two blocks east of that picket-fenced lawn is a wooded bluff overlooking the duck ponds and grassy lawns of Woodland Park. The ponds are fed by a brushy river. The river leads north out of town into farmland. The farmland eventually gives way to timber. Beyond that is Glacier National Park, cougar heaven. Walk any city. Look for a brushy trail into town via railbeds, riverbanks, and parks through which a wary animal could move unnoticed. If the trail is there, and big game roams outside the city, it roams the city, too.

And that's why a cougar that wandered into a city might stay. Cougars cannot subsist long on small game. It takes a lot of protein to keep a cougar fit. Cities that harbor deer—and most do— provide that. City residents ensure a healthy deer population with flower beds, green lawns, and even the salt blocks they use to bait deer into their yards, a practice Jim Halfpenny calls "chumming for lions."

The people who mediate between cougars and their unwitting hosts are game wardens like Ray. As wardens learn to hunt urban backyards for cougars, painful experience teaches them they must also manage the owners of those backyards. Jerry Brunham, the grizzled game warden in Nanaimo, British Columbia, believes there are things people don't want to hear when they phone in a sighting. They don't want to know that cougars are here to stay until we kill them, starve out the in-town deer, and log off every in-town thicket where a cougar could hide.

He knows he can't protect people from every cougar, but callers don't want to hear that, either. What he's learned is that people will insist he respond to a sighting, but that he not shoot the cat. People don't want blood on their hands, and they don't realize that relocation is often just slow killing. Brunham has learned that people think cougars are endangered, and therefore every one should be spared. He's right in his assumptions just often enough to hang onto them, even though they make his job nearly impossible.

Here's how game wardens learn these assumptions.

Jerry once shot a cougar that had been on a sheep-killing spree near a popular hiking trail on the edge of Victoria, capital city of the province. Next thing he knew, a woman wrote to the *Victoria Times-Colonist* to say, "We pay conservation officers to help save animals, not kill them. I think it's awful that a conservation officer would shoot and kill a cougar that could have easily been tranquilized and moved somewhere else... I think that the conservation officer who shot it for no particular reason should be charged and definitely should not have this job. He should work in a slaughterhouse."

That nasty letter was nothing compared to what happened to Ray Kahler the day his game warden assumptions failed everyone— Ray himself, a stray cougar, and the public he serves. Ray's bad day started at 6:00 A.M., as he was gathering gear for a day off. He'd planned to hunt turkeys in the mountains north of Spokane. Across town, South Hill residents had spotted a cougar prowling near Manito Park. A dozen Spokane police cars were dispatched to scour the neighborhood. Then the police called Ray, herder of parking-lot moose, trapper of downtown bears.

Up on South Hill, it's easy to forget Spokane's grimy industrial heart: the smelters and railyards that built the city. Tree-lined streets with quaint older homes radiate out from the duck pond and grassy glens of Manito Park into a *Sunset* magazine cityscape.

Swinging down from his truck at the impromptu police command post, Ray found a circus. Patrolmen's radios squealed out reports, dispatchers relayed orders, and officers in cruisers hustled pedestrians off the sidewalks. Two sniper teams in full regalia were standing by. The only performer missing was the cougar: police hadn't located it.

Ray shook his head. If they just waited, the animal would probably go to sleep in a quiet spot and then sneak away. He was relieved when it became apparent that the police were running out of patience. He agreed that their patrol cars could be put to better use in downtown traffic. The search could be continued by a team of police volunteers.

Ray headed home to grab his turkey gear.

His phone rang again a little after 9:00 A.M. The cat had treed near the corner of Tekoa and 26th. Ray knew the cougar had lost its chance to slip out of town. This time, expecting an even larger crowd and some attention from his superiors at Fish and Wildlife, he put on his olive-and-tan uniform before heading out.

Ray knew his choices: shoot the cat on the spot or dart it with tranquilizers and relocate it. Ray would agree with his colleague,

Jerry Brunham: there's nothing humane about relocation. It's easy
on the public but hard on cougars. One reason wardens relocate
cougars is because they're pretty sure people don't want to face that
truth. They're very sure we aren't willing to let the cougar go its own
way. If we were, we wouldn't call to complain in the first place.

When Ray pulled through the police line, it looked like a sce-
nario from the sergeant exam. Police were trying to hold back a
crowd of one hundred people. All three TV stations were on
hand, cameras running. Three snipers, two in full SWAT gear,
were stationed at the base of a Ponderosa pine. Forty-five feet
above them all, a big tom cougar stared down from a stout limb.

"Here we go," Ray thought.

Police told him their orders were to shoot the cat if it came out
of the tree. Ray looked at the crowd, the faces in windows, and
the rows of homes marching down 26th. A bullet could do a lot
more damage here than a cougar.

Across the street, one of the TV crews was having a shoving
match with a couple of beat cops. It looked like the reporters
were being arrested. Ray, meanwhile, waited for the veterinarian
to arrive with the tranquilizer. The cougar was getting twitchy, the
way they do when they're looking to run again. This was turning
into what cops call "a situation."

By the time the vet arrived, Ray had been envisioning worst
cases for an hour. The cougar leaping down, panic-stricken, and
bowling into a child. Police spraying bullets down 26th at a scam-
pering cat. The anesthetic, never completely reliable, putting a
confused and angry cougar on the ground with 100 people. He
needed a safe, bloodless outcome the public could stomach. The
cougar needed to die—it was the kindest thing anyway—but it
couldn't be shot from that tree.

"I want you to OD this cat," Ray said quietly to the vet.

The vet didn't argue. He loaded a lethal dose in his tranquilizer
gun, but missed his first shot. The cat startled at the ping of the
dart hitting a nearby branch, and climbed higher. By now, the vet
was in a hurry. He slammed in a second hypo and shot. A clean

Spokane police were unnerved when a cougar took refuge on residential South Hill in this large tree, later dubbed the "Puma Ponderosa."

hit. The cat crept out to the weak end of its limb, slipped and toppled to the ground, groggy but still on its feet. Ray didn't let out his breath until it settled onto its haunches, convulsed, and lay still.

"Good job," a voice called from the crowd. Considering how wrong it could have gone, Ray was thinking so, too, despite the fact that he was loading an overdosed cougar into the back of his truck. Other voices asked how long the cougar would be unconscious, where he'd be taken, whether he'd be all right. Ray told them what he assumed they wanted to hear: a lie. When it recovered, he said, the cougar would be freed in the wilderness.

Then Ray Kahler drove back to the Fish and Wildlife office on Division Street, expecting the cat to be dead by the time he arrived. Instead, it was banging off the walls of its box.

Ray told his boss the whole story. If he expected to be commended for engineering a palatable ending, he was disappointed. Mike Whorton was unhappy that Ray had opted to kill the cat, unhappier still that he had lied. One of the agency's rules is that cougars must pose a threat before they are killed. The cat had been up a tree. What harm could it do there? Soon, Ray found himself trying to argue his boss and another office-type into his point of view: There had been too many police with guns drawn, too many onlookers, and a cat fixing to make a dash. They weren't buying it.

And they didn't like his solution to the new problem any better. "What would be more humane?" Ray asked. "Giving it a shot there in the back of the truck, or releasing it to die in the woods?"

They weren't budging. Ray had promised people the cat was going to be released. It had to be released, even if it was almost certainly dying.

Ray volunteered to take it. At an arranged drop-off spot, he spilled the cat from its cage and watched it walk, shakily the way a drugged cat does, to a log where it was resting when Ray drove away. He began to think it might survive. A few hours later, uncertain why it suddenly mattered, he returned to check on the animal. If he was hoping to find it gone, he was disappointed. The cat was lying near where he'd left it. It was dead.

"Agent lied—they meant to kill cougar" came the page-one headline a week and a half later. Somehow, the newspaper had found out.

Bruce Smith, the Spokane region director of Washington Fish and Wildlife, issued a public apology. It didn't offer even token support for his veteran sergeant. He announced an investigation into whether Ray should be fired or otherwise reprimanded. Letters to the editor stung Ray so badly that he took time off work to hide out. Tina Bjorklund, in whose front yard the cougar had treed, hung a sign—"The Puma Ponderosa"—and told *Spokesman-Review* reporter Adam Lynn, "I don't like the people I pay taxes to lying to me like that."

Ray Kahler still wears the olive-and-tan uniform of Washington Fish and Wildlife in Spokane. But just barely. He looks forward to retiring, and back with nostalgia on the days when wildlife officers did their jobs in the wild. It was easier. It made sense. Until people decide whether and how to live with cougars in their cities, a guy like Ray has a hard, hard job.

9

Danger in the Santa Anas

San Juan Creek, near San Juan Capistrano, California, where five-year-old Laura Small was snatched by a cougar in 1986.

Sue Small turned around. Her daughter was gone.

"Laura?"

There was no sound. Standing alone in the stream, Sue thought for a moment she'd imagined the cougar. There had been no growling, no snarling, and no yelling, just a flash of brown that grabbed her five-year-old by the head and climbed the bank, the child's small hands prying at its jaws. Now there was only the clucking of the stream, a few bugs buzzing, and the smell of slow water on a warm day.

Sue yelled louder. "Laura!"

It was March of 1986. Sue and her husband Don had driven into the foothills of Southern California's Santa Ana Mountains with Laura and their nine-year-old, David. Interstate 5 had been crowded with people headed to nearby San Juan Capistrano's annual Swallow Day celebration.

At the gate to Ronald W. Caspers Wilderness Park, which the family visited regularly, they were given the official map. It warned visitors to be careful of the most dangerous form of life in the park: poison oak.

The Smalls hiked north on a popular nature trail to San Juan Creek, where Sue and Laura took off their shoes to hold hands and wade in the shallows. Father and son grew bored and headed a little farther up the canyon.

"Why don't you go over to the edge of the stream and see if you can see the tadpoles now?" Sue told Laura, letting go of her hand. She watched her little girl, in white shorts and a blue tank top with butterflies on it, slosh away through the ankle-deep water. As Laura bent to dip her plastic cup in the stream, Sue thought she saw something move toward her daughter. She turned, looking for a dog. It was a cougar. A cougar? Before she could react, Laura was gone.

Sue called Laura's name, struggling to disbelieve the awful image: her baby had not, had absolutely not just been snatched by a wild animal. When the child didn't answer, Sue believed. She screamed so hard she bent over with her hands on her knees to empty her lungs.

Don and David reappeared.

"A mountain lion has Laura. I don't know where they are," Sue yelled. Then they were gone again.

Sue splashed to the bank. Her penny loafers lay next to Laura's tiny sneakers. Reality slipped again. Wasn't this still a perfect sunny Sunday, Sue playing piano for the church choir, then a family hike? Things like this didn't happen in St. Louis, where Sue grew up.

Laura moaned, somewhere close by. Sue pivoted and ran blindly up the streambank, scrambling over cacti and boulders. She nearly stumbled on the cougar. It stared at her, Laura hanging from its jaws by her neck. The child's head flopped forward like a rag doll's. Blood ran down her arms and onto the ground. The cougar never blinked.

Sue screamed again, this time making words, "Help! Somebody help me!"

A man appeared from the hiking trail to her left, told her to wait while he got a gun, and then ran away.

Next, a slim, dark-skinned man ran up, cracked a limb off a manzanita bush and started shouting at the cougar and stabbing at its eyes. The cougar batted the sharp stick away with one front paw. A confused moment later, the man was barking at Sue, "Grab your baby and run!"

She snapped to. The man now stood between the cat and Laura, who had been dropped in a motionless heap. Sue gathered her up and spun away, her daughter's mangled head cradled against her shoulder. She nearly ran into her husband. He draped his jacket over the child and they began to run.

David had found a ranger, who met them in a jeep somewhere near the trailhead. "Don't worry, she'll be OK," the ranger said as he propped Laura up in the seat.

"No," Sue thought to herself. "Don't tell me that. She's going to die."

An eye surgeon, a plastic surgeon, a neurosurgeon-and a trauma expert worked on Laura for fourteen hours. The neurosurgeon told Sue he'd never seen head wounds that bad. Laura's skull was crushed. A chunk of bone was missing. Her left eye couldn't be saved. But Sue had been wrong. Laura made it.

When Laura left the hospital five weeks later, she had no control of her right side. She couldn't walk. A steel plate patched the hole in her skull. She wore a bike helmet to protect the knitting bones as she stumbled around the house trying to make her body obey.

Orange County closed the park. A male lion was shot 400 yards from the attack site. The county's board of supervisors had a tough choice to make. Was that kind of lightning likely to strike again, ever? Biologists said no, but had to admit that you couldn't be sure unless you were willing to kill every cat in the area.

The park closure was not popular. About a month after the attack, the park reopened, with extra cougar warning signs in place.

Ronald W. Caspers Wilderness Park is not very wild. White people drove the Juaneño Indians out of the foothills two hundred years ago so the settlers could raise cattle there. Later, a 7,600-acre ranch remnant along San Juan Creek was set aside as Caspers Wilderness Park. Now San Juan Capistrano and neighboring cities are steadily surrounding it as they move up the canyons toward the Santa Ana Mountains. Just like other foothills parks in the Santa Anas though, the dry scrublands and canyon oak forests are full of deer. That makes them wild enough for cougars.

Seven months after the attack, the Smalls sued Orange County and the California Department of Fish and Game. They argued that officials had been negligent for failing to warn park visitors that between September of 1985 and March of 1986, there had been seven daytime sightings of unusually bold cougars, about one a month. Three weeks before the attack on Laura, a woman had been stalked by a lion that would not leave until she pelted it with rocks.

And then, less than two weeks after the Smalls filed suit, lightning struck again in Caspers.

Tim Mellon carried his dream of a backwoods life in the sheath knife he wore on his hip. Paved and populous Southern California was just a place to make good money working construction until the family could move to the mountains. He and his brother-in-law, Bill, scouted flea markets, collecting ever-bigger knives to match their ever-bigger dreams.

On October 19, Tim and Bill drove their families up the Ortega Highway to Caspers Wilderness Park. They left the two vehicles at a dusty trailhead. Hiking up the oak-canopied trail, Tim thought the park looked like the woodsy countryside where he hoped to live one day. The pack of children led, all except Tim's son Justin, who had stopped to tie his sneakers. The tow-headed six-year-old was just learning his knot, so it often came undone. The other adults passed by, but Tim waited for Justin to finish. Then he watched the boy run around a curve to catch the other kids.

As the adults neared the next hairpin turn, Tim heard children screaming. Justin's sister, Aimee, came around the corner first, pale, still screaming, and running all-out for the car. The other kids were close behind. Justin wasn't with them.

As Tim ran, his first thought was that some pervert had grabbed the boy. He'd read about bodies ditched along the Ortega Highway. Bad stuff happened out here from time to time. He rounded the bend and found his stepbrother James, frozen in place, staring at something obscured by trailside brush. A few more steps and Tim saw the cougar. It straddled Justin, its hind legs on either side of his head. It bit at Justin's legs. The boy, pinned on his back, fiercely kicked and squirmed.

Tim couldn't make himself move. He was no match for this thing. It was huge, all muscles, teeth, and thick fur. To him, it looked like the animal was toying with Justin like a little rabbit. Then the boy seemed about to scrabble free, but the cougar bit him again. For Tim, it was one time too many. Scared as he was, he yanked his knife from its sheath and moved in. The cougar grabbed Justin's head in its teeth and began dragging him farther into the thick brush. Tim raised his shaking hand to stab the cat, but it let go of the boy and moved a few feet away.

Staring at the cat, he picked Justin up and handed the boy to his wife, Anne, who had run up behind them. The cat's eyes followed the boy, but Bill appeared and stepped in beside Tim. The men raised their arms, screaming, "Get the hell out of here!"

The cougar stared a moment longer, then slowly turned and walked into the bushes.

The men hurried to catch up with Anne. When Justin was rolled into Tim's arms, the boy opened his eyes and looked up at his father.

"Dad, am I going to live?"

Justin was covered with blood. His surfer shorts and T-shirt were in shreds. His bare legs looked like hamburger. So did his head. No way he'd make it, Tim thought.

"Justin, you're going to live," he told him.

At the Mission Viejo Trauma Center, surgeons pieced Justin together with more than five hundred stitches. Tim pieced the kids' story together. They had read the park warning sign about poison oak and the notes on the map about rattlesnakes and cougars. They joked about it all through the hike. Justin was down on one knee tying his shoes again when he heard another kid yell, "Mountain Lion!" He thought it was a psych-out, but then something hit him so hard it knocked him out of his sneakers.

The cougar that attacked Justin Mellon in 1986 knocked him out of his shoes, as this police photo shows.

At Ronald W. Caspers Wilderness Park—scene of two cougar attacks—visitors are met at the gate by warning signs and updates on recent cougar sightings.

Before they left the hospital, a man approached Tim and introduced himself as a private investigator working for a lawyer up north. Did the family want a lawyer? By that night, the attorney representing Laura Small had signed up the Mellons, too. When the lawyer told Tim about the park's cougar incidents, Tim was furious. This was just like the movie *Jaws*, he thought, in which the government lied about danger to protect the tourist trade.

When the Mellons sued, their lawyers filed a picture taken at Caspers Wilderness Park the day before the attack. A mother hurries out of the frame, clutching her child. The toddler looks over her mother's shoulder, eyes locked on a well-camouflaged cougar, which stares intently back. Richard Staskus, the families' lawyer, argued that the county and state had failed to protect park visitors. Plus, he said, Orange County had encouraged rapid development in the foothills without regard for possible impacts on cougar habitat and behavior.

Orange County's board of supervisors closed the park again. What else could they do? Biologists were assuring them the attacks were bad luck, pure and simple. Cougar attacks were incredibly rare. But lawyers for the county argued that if another child were attacked, Orange County would be slaughtered in court, no matter what a hundred biologists said.

The park cautiously reopened three months after Justin's attack. Children were restricted to picnic areas in the paved-road section. Families with children were not allowed to camp overnight. Cougar warning signs were installed at trailheads and parking lots, and rangers posted handwritten reports after each sighting. Visitors were required to sign liability waivers.

When Laura's case went to trial, jurors were shown a videotape of a lovely happy child dashing after a pet bunny. The tape of Laura after the attack captured a frustrated, disfigured five-year-old fumbling with blocks and crashing about in her helmet. Jurors heard about cougar sightings and confrontations leading up to the attack, looked over park handouts with the jocular warning about poison oak, and awarded the Smalls $2.1 million. The county's lawyer had argued that wild animals were unpredictable and the county couldn't be expected to protect everyone from every possible risk. The jury disagreed. People expected the government to protect them in a county park. The county gave up and quietly settled with the Mellons for about $100,000.

Caspers remained mostly off-limits to kids for more than a decade.

Meanwhile, Justin grew up to be a football star. He read everything he could find about cougars. He figured he got attacked because he was just in the wrong place at the wrong time. Laura learned to walk again and hiked in Caspers and other Santa Ana foothills parks. Although blind in one eye, she became a painter who sometimes produced polemical canvases in favor of wildlife preservation. People had overstepped their bounds, she thought, pushing too far into the cougars' turf. Justin's and Laura's attitudes were common in California, a state that even after these and other attacks repeatedly upheld the strongest cougar protections in the West.

Orange County reopened Caspers Wilderness Park to kids on December 16, 1997. Less than two weeks later, two women hiking in the park with young children were rushed by a cougar. Nobody was injured.

"We have to decide if this is a park for children to play in or a park for mountain lions. The two are not compatible," protested County Supervisor Charles Smith. But the county wasn't prepared to make another unpopular decision. They had been heavily criticized for the earlier closures, and there was no way the public would tolerate cougar extermination. They'd cross their fingers and hope for the best.

The cougar was shot. The park remains open to children. There have been no more attacks.

10
Demise of the Santa Ana Cougar

Scientists say the cougars of Southern California's Santa Ana Mountains are doomed by roads and rampant development.

Cougar attacks can have lasting repercussions, particularly attacks on children. Laura Small and Justin Mellon's injuries precipitated one of the most in-depth cougar studies in California history. Suddenly, everyone wanted to know what was going on with Santa Ana cougars.

Researchers followed a total of thirty-two radio-collared cats over five years. What they uncovered surprised almost everyone. The study was partly designed to evaluate human risks, but what it showed most clearly was that, even in a state that allowed no hunting, humans were far more lethal to cougars than vice versa. In fact, the Santa Ana cougars were dying.

The Santa Anas are the north end of a series of coastal ranges running from near Disneyland in Orange County to the Mexican border 135 miles south. From the freeways, you can see the steep and brushy peaks riven by oak-filled canyons. Saddleback, the Santa Anas' highest point, is dramatic at 5,687 feet, but not high enough to capture and hold water-storing snowfields, so most streams on the west slope of the range run only sporadically. Low in the remaining undeveloped foothills canyons, chapparal grass, sagebrush, and manzanita thrive in crunchy, sterile-seeming granitic soils. The Santa Anas feel wild, the kind of place cougars belong.

But, the study asked, were the Santa Anas wild enough, and if not, could cougars adapt?

One morning, a tracker trailed a cougar to her grassy daybed in a small canyon northeast of Laura Small's hometown, El Toro. Bulldozers growled into view, punching a new road through the grassland. The street sign was already in place: Antonio Parkway, it said. To the north, the tracker could see golfers on the new Rancho Margarita. From across the canyon came the gunfire din of hammers building a hundred homes in Mission Viejo. A half-mile south, heavy equipment roared, gouging out the foundations of a new canyon bridge and another road into the Santa Anas.

On another day, graduate student Dave Choate watched a young male cougar rest in open ground near a well-used jogging and biking trail. That night, two people climbed a ridge above the cat to watch the Disneyland fireworks show in nearby Anaheim. After the show, they walked home, oblivious to the cougar that watched from 200 yards away.

The Santa Ana cougars were so discreet that people barely noticed them. Why couldn't the two coexist indefinitely?

The eighth male collared in the study was nineteen months old when his mother abandoned him in a dry canyon. Midway through his second week alone, the young male made his first big kill, a mule deer fawn that he fed on for three nights. It was an auspicious start.

He soon found a temporary home range at Trestles Beach, just down the coast from San Clemente. Trestles offers world-famous waves and a lonely vibe: rocky sand, empty bluffs, and no houses, hotels, or state park hordes. Surfers have to hike in from I-5. The animal found a thick willow forest at the mouth of a creek where he could sleep by day. Nearby were plenty of small game to augment a beginner's diet.

Shortly after they parted ways, his mother was killed by a car on I-5. When the young male left the surfer hangout, he passed through her now-vacant territory and continued north, wandering the open scrubby ridges above San Juan Capistrano, hunting the grasslands around the city dump, walking through a commercial nursery, and then resting near the city sewage plant one night.

In time, he climbed the flank of the Santa Anas via a mostly dry creekbed on the city limits of Mission Viejo. Over the years, Beier's team would track several cats up the same canyon. In places, houses are built right up to its steep banks. Where there weren't homes, there were often bulldozers carving out new homesites on the rim.

During the day, the young cougar lay in thick brush near trails used by hikers, joggers, and dirt bikers. It was perfect ambush cover, but he never showed himself, never bothered anyone that Beier heard of. Finally, he moved north again, and crossed a freeway into the Chino Hills, where a state park and some private ground remained undeveloped. Since the study team hoped to document and encourage the crossbreeding of cougars in the Santa Anas and the Chino Hills, that looked to them like success.

But the radio collar stopped transmitting and Beier's crew lost track of the Trestle Beach cat. A month later a stalled motorist stumbled on the cougar's carcass in a weedy ditch in Pomona. A city of 132,000, Pomona is surrounded by other Los Angeles suburbs: Ontario, San Bernardino, Riverside, and Santa Ana. The cougar had to have crossed subdivisions and many roads to reach the spot where an auto killed him, 30 miles from the crest of the Santa Ana Mountains, far from the last open ground in the foothills.

In the fall of 1990, Beier and his crew collared a young male cougar treed by neighborhood dogs in Temecula on the east side of the Santa Anas. He wound up far down the foothills in a busy little canyon park just east of Santa Ana, a city of 300,000. The canyon winds through a thickly settled neighborhood, but there were enough deer and smaller prey for the cougar to gain 15 pounds. He spent his days resting in the densest part of the willow forest, a few feet from passing hikers and bikers.

He moved on, as young cougars do when seeking a permanent home. As he climbed back toward the crest of the Santa Anas, he crossed a commuter shortcut called Santiago Canyon Road and was hit by a car. The collision broke both hind legs. The young cougar had to drag himself a quarter of a mile to find shelter in a wooded canyon. There was a small spring there, but for the first week, the cougar was unable to crawl to it for a drink. About two weeks after the accident, trackers found an opossum carcass, probably the injured cat's first meal.

Another week passed. The cougar limped south 2 miles to a small reservoir popular with residents of an adjacent subdivision. There was a willow forest to hide in and plenty of water. For about three weeks the cougar lived a few dozen yards from subdivision homes, dogs, and people. The wounded cougar limped very short distances each night, sticking to easy, level terrain. Beier's team found only opossum carcasses, a bad sign, since small game normally only supplements a diet of bigger game like deer. There were only two reported sightings.

About five months after the car hit him, the young male had made his way back to the little canyon where he had lived well in his first weeks after leaving his mother. He lay down in a willow thicket there and died. The three-year-old weighed 82 pounds, a fraction of what he should. Beier found that the car had broken the cougar's right thigh bone just above the knee. Massive scar tissue had rebuilt the leg. But it turned backward a quarter turn and canted out 20 degrees. The cat's left thigh bone had broken off right at the ball. That left him without a solid connection between his leg and the rest of his body. For months, the cougar had hunted and traveled with the two broken ends grinding against each other.

In all, twelve radio-collared and seven uncollared cougars were hit by cars between 1988 and 1992. Each year, more than half of the kittens and a quarter of the study adults died, many of them hit by cars. Only two in ten kittens would live to adulthood. The young adults searching for a home range were most at risk. It seemed roads and highways were one thing the Santa Ana cats could not adapt to.

Meanwhile, the human population of Orange County could easily have thought there were more cougars than ever. Cougars were showing up in backyards and parks and at school bus stops. One even made it into downtown Oceanside, a city of 128,000. This cat, the eleventh male collared by the research team, was abandoned by his mother near San Juan Capistrano, and then headed south into undeveloped land on Camp Pendleton. There, he was hit by a car in early 1992.

Beier's trackers found a blood splatter on the road, but it must have been a minor injury, because the radio signals showed that the cat rested for just two days before traveling down the coast toward the San Luis Rey River. The river corridor is a thin thread of green brush with houses sporadically clustered along it. One night the cougar walked under the I-5 bridge and followed the river into the sleeping town. It was a fatal mistake.

Just before 3:00 A.M. on February 29, Oceanside Police Sgt. Rick Anthony was flagged down by a man who said he'd just seen a cougar on the beach. Soon there were more sightings. When Anthony spotted the big cat, it was dashing through the grounds of an apartment building and up a staircase onto a nearby road bank. Police aren't paid to ignore possible hazards, so they closed in on the cat.

State animal control officers, more accustomed to catching dogs and housecats, failed to snare the cougar on the road bank. It escaped into another apartment complex. By then, there were eight police officers, three animal control officers, and an apartment security guard in on the chase. They surrounded the apartment building. While the animal control officers searched the interior, a security guard called to say the cat was on the roof. The police officers on the ground spotted it jumping from balconies to rooftops, northbound.

By now, the city was waking up. Anthony and his colleagues decided capture was going to be nearly impossible. It was time to shoot the cat, before anyone got hurt.

When the cougar was located again, Anthony lined up four officers and ordered them to shoot with him on the count of three. They did, but the cat still bolted toward a Fish and Game officer. He fired a sixth shot. The cat turned and ran. The officers followed blood spots up the street.

A few blocks away, they found the cougar holed up under a porch. Sergeant Anthony, on one side of a 5-foot fence about 20 feet from the cougar, aimed at its head and fired. The cougar ran straight at him. Anthony fired nine more shots. The cougar fell at the other side of the fence. The Fish and Game officer fired one final round behind the cat's ear.

There is no mention of the cat's 1-pound radio collar in Anthony's report, nor of any attempt to call Beier's research team, who had the experience to deal with awkward cougar situations.

Consider the odds on replacing that one adult cat shot in Oceanside. For starters, two or three females would have to be bred, something not to be taken for granted, since the team had documented years in which fertile females went unbred in the Santa Anas.

Once bred, the hypothetical pair of females would have to beat the one-in-four odds against annual adult survival and give birth

Photo by Bob Wiesner

Odds of a one-month-old kitten in the Santa Anas surviving its first year are one in five.

to five kittens. Four of the five kittens would probably die in the first year. One would survive, but while he was growing to adulthood, his potential territory would shrink with every new homesite notched into the foothills of the Santa Anas.

Despite the adaptability of individual cats, the Santa Ana cougar population as a whole was fragile in the face of such rapidly shrinking habitat. During the study's final years, the six counties of Southern California contained 5 percent of the U.S. human population. The cities bordering the northern Santa Anas were on pace to double in fifteen years to about 2.3 million people. The 8.8 million people of Los Angeles were spreading south toward the growing suburbs of San Diego, population 2.5 million.

Biologists have learned that it takes a certain number of breeding animals to maintain a population. In the Santa Anas, Beier calculated, that number was at least two dozen. Two dozen adults and the youngsters in their orbits would need 1,400 square miles of open land. By 1993, undeveloped lands in the Santa Anas totaled just 1,287 square miles. Only half of these lands were protected from development.

Beier thought the cats might yet survive if people were willing to preserve narrow corridors of undeveloped ground connecting bigger patches like beads on a string. Could such a necklace substitute for a single large tract of habitat?

After the study concluded, conservation groups did succeed in buying up some ground to preserve wildlife corridors. But ultimate success would have meant cooperation among the seventeen cities and five counties ringing the Santa Ana Mountains, the Chino Hills, and the Santa Margaritas. All of those towns compete for new housing and the jobs that come with growth.

By late 1999, there was little support for the now extraordinary efforts that would be required to keep cougars in the Santa Anas. Steve Torres, the biologist in charge of California's cougar program, took the weary tone of a doctor waiting for a family to unplug a loved one on life support. Only through artificial and temporary means such as transplantation would the Santa Anas continue to be home to cougars, Torres said. Transplantation would be a likely death sentence for any cat you moved in. There are too many roads. There is no longer enough habitat.

11
Imagine It's Your Child

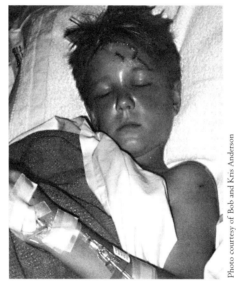

Joel Anderson, 11, recuperating from a cougar attack in a Lewiston, Idaho hospital.

Judy Underdahl stopped the motor home to photograph the cougars lying under a tree. They looked as bored and sleepy as her father, Pete, dozing in the back seat. He wanted to get home to Minnesota, but had humored her wish to detour through a Rapid City, South Dakota animal park called Bear Country.

"They look like they're dead," Judy said to her mother, Hazel. Judy handed Hazel the camera. "Will you clean your lens? I can't even see the cougars."

"I wanna see," shouted Judy's tow-headed two-year-old. Jason jumped on the upholstered engine cover to Judy's right.

At the toddler's shout, one of the cougars pricked up its ears, eyed the boy, and ran to Judy's window. Its front paws thumped against the side of the motor home.

"It's coming in," Judy whispered, but no one heard her. Often unnerved by cows and even cats and dogs, Judy was terrified by the cougar's huge unblinking eyes and its loud purring. "It's coming in," she said again. Nobody heard.

She tried to shake it off by easing the motor home forward, but then the window slid open. In an instant, the cat had vaulted in, scrambled over Judy, knocked Jason on his back and pinned him to the engine cover.

Judy jumped to grab him, but the cougar bit her hand and flung it aside. The motor home crashed to a stop against a fence. Hazel backed further into the passenger seat corner, shouting "Get a knife, get a knife."

Instead, Grandpa Pete tried to choke the cougar. It bit him, then went back to biting Jason's neck and skull.

"Get a knife! Get a knife," Judy and Hazel screamed. The cougar shook Jason like a floppy toy. Pete stepped back, jerked open a drawer in the galley and rushed forward to give the knife to Hazel.

"You do it," he said.

"You do it," Hazel shouted back.

"Just do it!" Judy thundered, and Hazel seized the knife and plunged it into the cougar's chest just behind its left leg. She kept stabbing until the cougar dropped Jason and crawled onto the driver's seat to die.

Cougars are captivated by children. Like the Bear Country cat snapping to life when Jason's head popped up, caged cougars ignore passing adults but crash into the mesh when a child runs by. Sheba, the captive-born cougar at the Fund for Animals shelter east of San Diego, does that. She all but ignores adults, but stalks children who walk the path around her grassy pen.

Less than half of recent attack victims are children, but that statistic masks this one: when a cougar singles somebody out of a mixed-age group, it chooses a child. This disturbs parents and policy makers both. It should.

The cougar that walked into a campground in British Columbia's Okanagan Valley in 1993 found a boy and his father panning gold. It leaped on the boy. So did the cougar who, on the bank of Washington State's Dungeness River in 1994, encountered a five-year-old and his dad throwing rocks in the water.

Like these kids, the likeliest child victim is a boy. He's older than four, but younger than twelve. He's rarely alone when attacked. Adults or other kids are close enough to save his life, but their presence does not prevent the attack. Most of his wounds, concentrated around head and neck, occur as the cougar tries to drag him away, just as it would a deer. No matter how fast rescuers move, the cougar will have moved much, much faster. The child's injuries will be life-threatening. The scars will be permanent.

Imagine this typical attack victim is your son. You leave him for just a moment. That's all Robert Anderson did. He climbed down a sandbar to the edge of Idaho's Salmon River, leaving his eleven-year-old son Joel and Joel's friend playing above him. Nine other people relaxed and played on the same sandbar. Then Robert heard his boy scream. He scrambled back up the bank to see a cougar biting Joel on the head and arm. Robert charged, letting his momentum power a punch to the cougar's nose that rolled it off the boy. It righted itself quickly and faced him, snarling. He kicked sand into its eyes until it ran away. Robert had moved fast, but Joel still needed eighty stitches.

Even worse, imagine you haven't left your child for an instant. You're right there, but that doesn't save him. When a bold cougar was spotted in Mesa Verde National Park in July of 1997, rangers began escorting hikers out of the area. Rafael DeGrave, a four-year-old French boy, was with his family and a ranger when he spotted the cougar several feet from the trail. He screamed and ran. The cougar immediately chased down the fleeing boy, grabbed him by the head, and dragged him into the bushes. Rafael's face and shoulder were ripped open before the family could drive the young cougar away.

Aaron Hall, sixteen years old, won a national heroism award for his quick reactions on July 31, 1998, at a day camp near Missoula, Montana. Dante Swallow, the smallest kid in camp, was shuffling up a hill at the end of a long line of hikers. He had fallen a step or two behind Aaron, the youngest counselor.

"There's a mountain lion," the six year-old said matter-of-factly.

When Aaron turned to look, he saw what appeared to be dog paws reaching up from behind the boy. Then something slammed Dante down, face first. When the animal locked its jaws on the boy's head, Aaron saw the eyes of a cat. He flashed on an old story: a boy snatched from his tricycle and killed by a cougar on the nearby Flathead Indian Reservation.

Aaron had no weapon, but somehow he knew he didn't need one. What he needed was an attitude. He rushed the cougar, kicking dirt in its face. It hooked its claws into Dante and began to drag him away. Aaron followed, booting the cat in the ribs until it shifted off the boy. Now Aaron stepped forward, straddling Dante just as the cougar had, glaring just as the cougar had. The cougar feinted at him, then reached in underneath to grab at the boy. Aaron kicked hard again, this time driving the instep of his worn-out running shoe into the cat's snout. It jumped up the road bank, but stopped 10 feet away to stare intently at Aaron. The teenager charged. A flick of tail and the cat was gone.

Dante is fine. The hero of the story, however, slept in his parents' room for three weeks. In his dreams, the boy was so little, the cougar so large.

Lila Lifely, another camp counselor, saved her young charge, too. But then she had to save her again. And again, as in a bad horror movie. Lila deserves every medal she got, three in all.

After hiking from YWCA Camp Thunderbird on the south end of Vancouver Island to a peak known as Crow's Nest, Lila and her handful of girls dropped their packs to celebrate the summit. The girls were playing a little way away in a clearing when Lila heard the first screams.

"Wild cat!" shrieked one girl as she passed Lila. "It's mauling Alyson!"

Lila raced to the little clearing. A cougar was dragging ten-year-old Alyson Parker by the head. Lila hit the cat on the forehead with a three-foot tree branch. The animal faded into the bushes.

She dropped to her knees beside Alyson. The girl was conscious and surprisingly calm. Her head wounds didn't look too bad, considering. Relieved, Lila ran for her pack to get first aid gear. Alyson moaned. Lila looked back. The cougar crouched over Alyson's head. Lila couldn't see what it was doing. She broke a four-foot long strip from a hollow log and clobbered the cat again. It shot away.

She whipped off her T-shirt and bandaged Alyson's head wounds with it. She had to have help but didn't dare leave. In desperation, she covered the child with a sleeping bag and heaped brush over that. Then she climbed a tree to holler for help. There she could keep an eye on Alyson and stay out of the cat's reach. The rest of the girls cowered in a group on the mountain's summit.

Lila didn't let her guard down until help arrived more than an hour later. But when the YWCA camp director knelt over Alyson to check her wounds, the campers screamed again. Lila snapped her head around to see the cougar crawling through the brush toward Alyson. Their shouting scared the cougar away long enough to get Alyson evacuated.

In May of 1985, twelve-year-old Johnny Wilson was camping on the west coast of Vancouver Island, just north of Camp Thunderbird, with his mother and two aunts. They sent him to the other side of a logjam to play with toy soldiers while they took a bath in the Darling River.

When he screamed, his mother, Alissa, and Aunt Deb sprinted

across the river. The cougar was huge, so big. Johnny's whole head seemed to have disappeared into its mouth. They grabbed the boy and the cougar let him go. Johnny's blood squirted 6 feet into the air with each heartbeat. Alissa knew only an artery pulsed like that. Johnny could be dead in minutes. The women concentrated on applying enough pressure to slow the bleeding but not enough to choke the boy. They ignored the cougar pacing circles around them, growling and snarling and sometimes leaning in with its muzzle just inches behind Alissa's head.

Seven hours later, a medic arrived from a U.S. Navy destroyer called to the scene. He checked Johnny's pulse and examined the awful neck and head wounds. He was sorry, he told Alissa. The boy was too badly hurt. He wasn't going to make it.

"Oh yes I am," said Johnny, sitting bolt upright. He was helicoptered off the beach to a Victoria hospital where he did make a complete recovery.

After a cougar attack, while their children are healing, parents spend years rebuilding their picture of the world and their place in it. In what kind of world is a child at risk of animal attack inside his grandpa's motor home? In what kind of world can a five-year-old be snatched almost out of her mother's hand? How should you raise a child in a world like that?

Millions of families go hiking every year without mishap. Rambunctious kids stray from the group and return, energized and confident to explore again. Statistics say the drive to the trailhead is the riskiest part of the trip. But what if you're the parent who picked the wrong trail at the exact, wrong moment?

On July 17, 1997, Dave and Kathy Miedema picked the trail to Cascade Falls, a popular seven-mile day hike on the west side of Rocky Mountain National Park. Lots of other people picked the same trail that day.

Ten-year-old Mark Miedema and his little sister Rachel were learning their parents' love of the high country. The family hiked and camped so often the neighbors called them "nature people."

On hikes, Mark seemed to play in every stream. Every few

moments, a different whatever caught his eye and he had to jump off the trail to take a closer look. Other times, he would run ahead to hide, then pop out from behind trees at his family, a broad smile cracking his freckled face.

The Miedemas and another family hit the Cascade Falls Trail a little after noon. They hiked past a paper sign posted at the trail-head:

WARNING!

MOUNTAIN LIONS

FREQUENTING THIS AREA

—BE ALERT—

SOLO HIKING AND <u>JOGGING</u> NOT RECOMMENDED, SUPERVISE
CHILDREN CLOSELY!
THIS IS MOUNTAIN LION HABITAT

MOUNTAIN LIONS ARE BEAUTIFUL AND POTENTIALLY DANGEROUS LARGE CATS THAT OCCUR IN THE PARK. ALTHOUGH RARELY OBSERVED AND NOT USUALLY A THREAT TO PEOPLE, HAZARDOUS ENCOUNTERS HAVE OCCURRED. UNSUPERVISED CHILDREN AND LONE ADULTS ARE ESPECIALLY AT RISK. INQUIRE AT VISITOR CEN-TERS FOR SAFE PRACTICES WHEN TRAVELING IN THE PARK.

At Cascade Falls, the family snacked on trail mix and granola bars. Their friends had turned back earlier. After a while, the Miedemas headed for their car as well. It was about 3:30. Mark was up to his usual explorations and nowhere to be seen. They met a backpacker who said the boy was three to four minutes ahead of them.

While Mark was doing his thing on that warm afternoon, a cougar was, too. She was 88 pounds, pregnant, and hunting. Moving along a ridge through thick aspens above a meadow, she was in the right spot to find deer, but what she found was Mark.

The first thing Mark's father saw were the boy's black Bermuda shorts and his skinny legs lying across the trail, his black socks and black sneakers unusually still. It could have been another of Mark's pranks, but there was a deer there. Or Dave thought it was a deer, until it picked Mark up by the head and dragged him down the trail.

Kathy saw it too, and they charged, screaming. The cougar dropped Mark and fled uphill into the trees. They ran to the motionless boy. He wasn't breathing. He had no pulse. They performed CPR with the help of a nurse who happened upon them. His heart fluttered once and quit again. They breathed for him and made his silent heart pump blood for nearly an hour. Then EMTs arrived to take over. Dave and Kathy gave their boy up to the coroner a little after 5:30.

The coarse hairs found on Mark's hands made the coroner think the boy had tried to fight back. But he was a 50-pound boy facing an animal that killed 100-pound deer for a living. The cougar had cracked the 10-year-old's skull, broken his nose, and had bitten and clawed his face, head, neck, arms, and chest.

Two years later, Kathy's brother says she still doubted her decision to let Mark run ahead and encounter the world at his own speed. She wrestled with her faith in God.

"We are slowly healing, although sometimes we take one step forward and two backwards," Dave wrote, on the first anniversary of Mark's death. He said they had yet to escape the cougar, which attacked them in memories, flashbacks, and nightmares.

They have ventured into the woods again. First, Dave and Kathy took Rachel on a quarter-mile hike. Little Rachel was bolder than her mother, Kathy later told her brother. But they came home safe, just as they had expected to the day Mark died, just as every other family hiking the park that day did.

12

Into the Jaws of Death

*Cindy Parolin was awarded Canada's Star of Courage
for saving her 6-year-old son from a cougar.*

Eleven-year-old Melissa Parolin loved riding horses. And she loved spending time with her mother, especially since time was something Cindy Parolin had precious little of. Melissa's mother had, until recently, juggled three jobs to pay off college loans, splitting her remaining energy among her husband and four children.

So on this August afternoon in 1996, Melissa didn't need the cool sun or high white clouds to make her smile. She sat straight-backed in the saddle, pretty Flicka's ears turned toward the base camp her father had picked out, from which the family would ride and explore for a glorious two weeks. Mum led the way.

Melissa rode often at her grandparents' ranch near the tiny British Columbia town of Tulameen. In fact, she couldn't remember the first time she had been lifted into a saddle. But the family had never gone on a horse camping trip before. Already they were miles from the ranch. Soon they would pass the last popular camping spots on the dirt Tulameen River Road. Then they'd have the woods to themselves.

Melissa was slim, brown-haired, and freckled, with gray eyes set wide in a round face. Her thirteen-year-old, lean-faced older brother, David, rode beside her with the same wiry athleticism that made him a hotshot in the hockey rink. Nine-year-old Billy, blond and good looking, rode before them.

Cindy, in the lead, was dark-haired like her daughter. When she smiled, round cheeks folded her dark eyes nearly shut. Like everyone else, Melissa found it hard not to smile back. But the best thing about Mum was that her sweet face and soft, round, 5-foot-1-inch frame concealed a rock-solid will. There were no problems Mum couldn't solve. You could tell she thought so, too.

All morning the family sauntered up the road, the cool air sparkling with jokes and laughter and bits of songs. Before they left the Parolin ranch, Grandma had said Cindy should carry a gun. Melissa didn't hear Mum's answer, but she wasn't troubled. Grandma was a worrier, always telling you to be careful about this or that. You'd think she still lived in the wild and woolly frontier of her girlhood.

The plan was for Dad to load a small mountain of food and camping gear into the bed of his old Ford half-ton. Meanwhile, Cindy and the three oldest children would ride more than 20 miles up seldom-traveled Tulameen River Road. Les would meet them at midday with lunch, and then drive ahead to set up camp at a cluster of run-down cabins somewhere near road's end. With Les was blond, bubbly Steven, six and too young for such a long ride. A family friend followed Les in Cindy's car. Cindy, juggling time as usual, needed the old Celica to drive into town for work several times during this adventure.

The day passed quickly, although the last few miles seemed much longer and dustier than the early ones. At 6:00 P.M., Melissa Parolin took a final sip of root beer and tossed the can. She didn't usually litter and wondered absently why she had. Then she forgot about the candy that a can refund could buy. She was tired and still hungry: Dad hadn't brought lunch. Instead he'd arrived with candy bars and pop just a few minutes ago. One candy bar for a whole day's ride? She was going to eat lots of dinner, that was for sure.

Now Dad was pulling ahead in a haze of dust. Billy rode beside him, drafted to help set up camp. Steven, rescued from the truck and thrilled as only a six-year-old can be at such a magnificent turn of events, rode placid old Goomba in Billy's place. He chattered excitedly about nothing, which, since he was by far her favorite brother, was only a little irritating. Melissa noticed that his sneakers were untied. The laces dangled toward the stirrups, which his short legs couldn't reach.

The road lay in shadow. The early evening air shimmered with the delicate, menacing hum of mosquitoes. Melissa pulled her jean jacket from the saddle tiedowns and slipped it over her bare arms. Mum said camp was minutes away. This sounded good to Melissa.

That was when movement caught her eye. Something popped out of the willows just left of the trail. It was brown and close to the ground: a head. Coyote, maybe. That was neat. You didn't see coyotes every day. Mum and Steven, unaware, pulled abreast of it, but the creature ignored them. It stared back down the road at Melissa. She stared back, puzzled. Coyotes were so shy. You mostly saw them running away. The ears and eyes flicked away from Melissa, lighting first on her mother, and then Steven.

As though that stare prickled, the lead horses sidestepped

nervously. Flicka stopped. Melissa could feel the big body tense between her legs. In the corner of her eye, she saw David's horse dance backward.

Just then, the brown animal began gliding onto the road. When its long tail emerged from the bush, Melissa understood this was no coyote. She was looking at a creature she'd seen only in books and on TV: a mountain lion.

Flicka's growing tension, Melissa knew, meant that in a few moments the horse would bolt. She had been thrown before. "Oh, no. This is going to hurt," came the thought.

Then, almost as absently, she realized she didn't have to be thrown. She could dismount. This she did, reflexively flipping the reins back over the animal's neck so the mare wouldn't trip if it ran. Moments later, she heard Flicka pound away.

Meanwhile, the cougar had slipped into the clearing off the road's right side, where Cindy and Steven now struggled to calm their jittery horses. Without a pause, it padded to Goomba's side and then rose straight into the air, where it seemed to float a moment before the little boy. Then it swiped a paw sideways. Melissa thought the motion looked like a person trying to clear a stack of books from a desk. The big paw missed, though, and the cougar dropped lightly to the ground.

"Hold on, Steven. Mum's coming. Hold on," Mum chanted.

But terrified old Goomba shivered sideways and Steven toppled toward the cat. He landed nearly at its feet, rolled once, and rose. Their heads seemed almost on a level. This time the boy was hard to miss. The cougar rose before him and stroked its front paws across his scalp. Instantly there was blood, a lot of it.

Melissa doesn't remember what Steven would later describe, that the cougar knocked him face-down, batted his head with its paws, and bit into his scalp. It felt to Steven as though the cat clawed slits in his scalp and then inserted its teeth into the incisions, delicately skinning him.

But Melissa was no longer watching her baby brother. She stared at her mom, who had dismounted and was breaking a branch from a log. The decisive crack freed her and she began hurrying forward. If Mum was doing something, maybe she, Melissa, could do something too.

Mum used the four foot-long stick to jab the cougar's shoulder, trying to push it from Steven, or at least distract it. It ignored her. She jabbed more fiercely. The stick snapped in two.

Then Cindy Parolin did something nearly unimaginable: this soft eastern Canada city girl threw herself full-length at the cat, rolled it off her son, jammed her right forearm into its mouth and pinned it on its back beside the bloody little boy.

This made more sense to Melissa than anything that had happened so far. Mum always took care of everything and everybody. The boy rose and stepped around his mother and the cat as though they weren't there. Silent, he walked into Melissa's arms and sagged against her. She slipped her arms under his and clasped her hands together.

The boy's face was almost untouched, with only one deep scratch across the nose. But the rest of his head was white and blue and pink, with flaps of bloody scalp hanging like tattered American flags. Even Steven's mutilated head didn't shake Melissa, though. Everything was going to be all right. Mum was in control.

Her mother lay motionless, concentrating on jamming her arm into the cat's mouth, keeping the back of its head pinned to the dirt. Melissa could see the slightly curved teeth press against the heavy fabric of Mum's oilskin riding jacket. Its front paws were planted against Cindy's chest. Its back legs were hidden beneath her body. Its tail lashed angrily, but it lay otherwise still, staring up at its captor. It didn't look so big now.

David appeared. Just as the snap of the stick had awakened Melissa, the sight of his mother tackling the cougar had unfrozen him. The thirteen-year-old was carrying a melon-sized rock.

"Do you want me to drop this on his head?"

"No," said Cindy. "It'll make him mad."

David didn't drop the rock where he stood. He walked away to replace it exactly where he'd found it. Melissa wished he were smashing it onto the cougar instead, but like all the Parolin children, David had been raised to mind.

Perhaps both children ticked through their options then. Les, a hunter and a cowboy, never went into the bush unarmed, but he and his gun were in camp. There was no knife, either. And no club. But there was was bloody little Steven, Mum with her arm jammed into a cougar's mouth, and a road that might remain empty for hours. All the horses were gone, their hoofprints tattooed into the road's clay surface.

"Take Steven and go get your dad," said Cindy.

Relieved to have a mission, Melissa shuffled onto the road, Steven a sagging weight in her arms. Then it dawned on her: every step left her mother more alone with the cougar. She glanced ahead. David had already disappeared down the road. She looked back. Her mother lay tensely atop the animal. It was still frozen except for the lashing tail. Everything was still under control. So why did her stomach feel like kneaded dough?

She turned and struggled down the road. Camp was minutes away, Mum had said before. Neither Melissa nor David knew exactly where, except that the cabins were away from the road. But luckily, Mum's car couldn't handle the steep sidetrack: it would be parked near the turnoff. They would find the car, it would point to Dad, and he would save Mum.

That was when she heard them: four or five long belly screams. It didn't sound like Mum, it sounded like an animal in pain. Melissa's calm snapped. Suddenly she understood that things were far from under control.

She needed to go back, but she also needed to do what she was told—find her dad. She froze. It was too much. Then a small voice piped up from the circle of her arms.

"Can I have your hat?" it said.

"What? Why?"

"So you don't have to see my head," Steven answered seriously. He had another reason, but he was too young to fit words to it. He could feel warmth slipping through the gashes in his head.

He thought when all the warmth snuck out, he'd be dead. If he could trap that life-warmth in his big sister's hat, he might live.

Melissa's attention snapped from her mother's danger to her little brother's. He was hurt bad. She pulled her prized cowboy hat from her head and placed it in his hands.

Beneath the hat, Melissa heard her brother mumble, "I'm kind of tired. Can I sit down?" This sleepy voice sounded even less like Steven. Melissa was tired, too. The boy's feet moved in front of her blunt-nosed cowboy boots, but she supported most of his weight.

There were no sounds from behind. That was almost worse than the screaming, but then the little voice came again, it said, "I feel tired. I have to sit down." A new fear struck her: Steven might be dying. It suddenly seemed clear to Melissa that a person missing so much scalp couldn't survive long. She guided him to a steep bank that might protect their backs.

"I have some raisins," said the voice.

"Eat them," Melissa ordered. Food might lend him strength. Steven's wanting food might be his body telling him how to stay alive. "Eat them."

And one by one, the boy pinched the shriveled fruit into his mouth, his blood-streaked face impassive.

Melissa didn't think she could carry him anymore. But it wasn't safe to sit here, and Steven needed a doctor. She began to yell, "David? David, I need help."

A few minutes later, David jogged back around the bend. "I saw the car," he said. But he'd been unable to find the camp. He told his sister he'd yelled for Dad and then yelled repeatedly, "Les!" so Dad wouldn't think somebody else's kid was calling. He punched the car horn, but it made no sound. He hunted for car keys, thinking he could drive back for Melissa and then Mum. There were none. Then he heard Melissa yell.

There were two places left to try. Beyond the car, the right fork of the road led to an abandoned hardrock mine. The left fork led to Myra Brewer's cabins. It was possible that the Parolin camp lay off one of those roads. It was also possible, though unlikely, that other people would be at the mine or at Myra's place.

David took his first good look at Steven then. The hat, he told his sister, should come off. It might get stuck to the wounds. Steven didn't resist as his big brother gently lifted it. Shocked by the flaps and folds of bloody scalp beneath, David found himself trying to push and pinch the mess back into place. The children let Steven rest a bit more. When they couldn't stand it any longer, each reached under an arm and lifted, letting the boy's feet shuffle on the road. Five minutes later, they reached Cindy's car.

David pulled a cooler out of the passenger side and Steven crawled in, folding himself into a bundle. The older children told him he was safe. They told him not to lock the door, so they could get in if he fell asleep, but Steven falling asleep wasn't what they were afraid of. Between the front seats lay an open pack of chocolate-covered Wagon Wheels. David thought Steven shouldn't eat anything, but Melissa again hoped food would make him stronger. Besides, Steven loved to eat.

"You can have some," she blurted, gesturing at the cookies. Usually you couldn't shut Steven up, but he didn't say anything. Melissa closed the door.

The children began yelling for their father. He had to be close. Maybe he'd hear two voices where he hadn't heard one. But their only answer was a shushing sound as wind caught in the upper branches of the pines. The slanted evening light pooled cool shadows on the road. It would be dark soon, and Mum was still alone with that cougar. Or worse, it had escaped her and watched them now from the leafy darkness that walled the road.

Someone needed to run up to the mine. They didn't want to leave Steven, but neither could stand to go alone. As they jogged uphill together, they didn't notice the twin tire ruts, faint and screened by brush, that veered left 100 feet from the car. Nor did they notice as they panted back down minutes later. Their mother needed help, but Melissa and David had failed to find any.

🦋

Fifty-one-year old Jim Manion and his wife Karen had arrived at their cabin Sunday night to begin a quiet vacation. Jim was tall. His angular features, stained-wood skin, and dark eyes bespoke his native Salish ancestry. His leg braces told of determination. After a tree fell on a much younger Jim, he had been told he'd never again walk. Now he wore shoes with heavy, stiff soles and weighty braces that ran up his calves to stabilize numb and mostly paralyzed feet. But by God, he walked.

Karen, forty-eight, was short and blond. Children liked her, perhaps because she liked them; in fact liked to think she had preserved in herself the best qualities of a kid. She hated shoes, so she seldom wore any. Barefoot now, she sat on the porch of the tiny, rough-cut lumber cabin Jim and two brothers-in-law had built.

That was when they heard something. Karen lowered her book. Jim tried to concentrate on the distant shouting. Children, he thought, but you couldn't hear the words. What were kids doing out here on a Monday evening? It would soon be dark. In a little while he'd go check it out, make sure nothing was wrong.

Minutes later as Jim returned from the outhouse, he saw a figure jogging into camp. He recognized the oldest Parolin boy, David. He didn't know the family except to nod at, but his grandparents and Les's had both moved to the area over a century ago. Jim's aunt, Myra Brewer, and Les's mother were friends.

The panting boy's story would have been hard to believe except for its matter-of-fact delivery. David sounded like he'd spent the last ten minutes arranging words into the most efficient order. Their mother needed help fighting off a cougar, little Steven was safe with Melissa in a car but was hurt, and David couldn't find his father, who was supposed to be nearby.

The boy's unflinching eyes pulled at Jim's heart and made him want to save the day even more than tears could have. The tall man clumped into the cabin and began throwing things onto the bed: towels for bandages, flour to slow bleeding, a jug of water to clean wounds, shells and his old 12-gauge shotgun.

The shotgun always leaned against the cabin wall. No longer used for hunting, it was simply a noisemaker to frighten off the occasional curious bear. This mountain lion was probably long gone, but just in case, Jim pulled the plug so the old shotgun would hold five shells instead of three.

Jim also threaded his bayonet-style hunting knife onto his belt. Then he scooped up the supplies and ran to the truck. Into the Chevy's back seat went his cow dog, Kala, and his brother-in-law's expensive young bird dog, a golden retriever named Trem, which the couple was babysitting. Jim's mind, ticking in high gear, could think of ways the dogs might be useful. He could hear Karen doing her kid magic by the truck. She encircled the boy with one arm, asking questions and listening gravely to the answers, helping David trust these adults he so desperately needed.

Melissa heard an engine. She had been feeding Steven boxed juice and cookies. She had read that badly injured people shouldn't be allowed to sleep, so she talked. She told him everything would be fine, even though she was now certain he was dying. The little boy seemed barely able to talk. All he said, when he spoke, was the refrain from that scary walk to the car, "I'm so tired."

After they had returned from the old mine, David had asked her to run up the remaining fork, toward old Myra Brewer's. He was tired. He'd already run a lot farther than she had.

"I can't go, David. I just can't," Melissa had begged. She was sick of being scared. All she could think about was climbing into Mum's car, slamming the door, and being safe. So they'd agreed that David would run one more time, as far as Myra's, then come back if he found no help. Nothing was said about what they'd do after that. What was there to say?

Melissa had climbed into the driver's seat beside Steven. A few minutes after David left, the urge to pee got so strong that she reluctantly got out. But once she was standing, the urge faded and she realized it was just fear pooling in her gut. She dove gratefully back into the car.

The white Chevy roaring up the road was a beautiful sight. Melissa jumped out and waved her arms. Two adults emerged with David. They were vaguely familiar.

The woman headed straight for Steven. She looked at the gelled red mess of his head, then checked the boy for less obvious wounds. Melissa couldn't hear her questions, but Steven's answers were tiny yeses and nos. When Karen backed out of the car, she seemed relieved. She said the bleeding had mostly stopped, the wounds looked worse than they were, and Steven would be all right. Then, before Melissa could relax into the reassuring authority of adults, the woman told her she would be staying with Steven again, alone.

Karen and her tall, stern-faced husband, Jim, needed David to find Cindy. Someone had to keep Steven from moving around, keep him in the car. Melissa bit back the words she wanted to yell, "No. Don't go. Don't leave me alone. You just got here."

She knew her disappointment showed, because the woman hugged her and said, "We'll be back. We'll be back as soon as we can."

Melissa climbed into the still-warm seat and shut the door. The truck bounced away and responsibility settled on her again. Beyond the window, she watched light slowly fade until the sky was dusky and deep. Time passed.

Then the roar of the truck came again. Melissa jumped out and anxiously scanned the cab, but only Jim, Karen, and David got out. Her question stuck in her throat a moment, then came out fast.

"Where's Mum?"

They told her a man with a blue van was taking Cindy to the hospital. Melissa relaxed a little. Mum was hurt—she had been braced for that ever since the screams—but hospitals fixed people who were hurt.

Karen explained that she and Jim would take them to the hospital, too. Jim wrote on a piece of paper, "Your wife has been injured. She was attacked by a cougar. Steven is seriously injured. They're being taken to the hospital."

He propped the note on the steering wheel and closed the door.

Melissa had another question, but they were loaded up and headed toward Princeton before she could make herself ask.

"How bad is she?"

Nobody answered, although Melissa gave them lots of time.

"How bad is she?" she asked again, louder and shriller.

David sounded reluctant, "It's fifty-fifty, Melissa. She's hurt pretty bad. Isn't that right, Jim?"

Fifty-fifty? What was that supposed to mean?

The ninety-minute drive to town was dreamlike. Steven rode in the woman's lap, his head wrapped in towels. Melissa was squeezed in back with David and two dogs. Somehow the woman got David talking about the movie *Star Wars*.

"Maybe we all know a song," the woman said, and the next thing Melissa knew, they were actually singing. Once, David stopped in the middle of a line he couldn't recall. A small voice piped from beneath the turban, finishing the line. Everyone laughed. For a grateful moment, Melissa forgot about fifty-fifty.

As Melissa stared beyond the adults' heads, she caught a glitter of silver and brown—her soda pop can from that afternoon. She even thought she saw a tiny tongue of dampness where the last drops of root beer had seeped out. She remembered how it had felt to toss the can aside, as though nothing she might do this day mattered all that much. She thought, then and years later, how odd it was that such a little thing, an empty pop can beside a dirt road, would stick so jarringly in her memory. If the day had ended as it was supposed to, she would have ridden by that pop can two weeks later, heading home with her entire uninjured family, and never noticed it.

And how had the day really ended? What had David and these

two adults found when they returned for Cindy Parolin? Melissa, caught up in fifty-fifty and too-well-remembered screams, didn't ask. Not that night, and not for a long time. And the stern-faced man behind the wheel, the only person who knew the whole, incredible story, thought it kinder not to offer.

13

Heroes

Photo courtesy of Similkameen News Leader, Princeton, British Columbia

Jim Manion and Karen Soule anticipated a quiet vacation at their cabin the night David Parolin appeared, asking for help for his wounded brother and embattled mother.

Jim Manion has waited years to tell the Parolin kids what really happened to their mom on the Tulameen River Road. But when the newspapers asked, he found he didn't want to talk to them. By his code, a man doesn't help his neighbor in order to win attention. The heroes were those brave kids and their brave mom. The newspaper stories should be about them.

The events of that Monday evening have not grown vague, however. From the moment young David jogged toward the cabin, Jim remembers everything, whether he wants to or not.

Jim, Karen, and the boy roared away from the Manion cabin to find the dusty brown Celica right where David had said it would be, more proof the boy was steady. While Karen tended the injured child, Jim examined the Parolin kids' faces. No tears. No panic. Even Steven, who looked like he'd been scalped, was dry eyed.

The boy shouldn't be moved. The bleeding might start again. Besides, Jim couldn't shake a vision of Cindy Parolin ripped to pieces in the road. He'd protect as many of the kids from that sight as he could.

Minutes later, David, Karen, and Jim scanned the road from the cab of his white Chevy. Pine- and willow-lined, rutted and rock-strewn, each turn looked the same to Jim. He drove slowly. Soon they would lose daylight, but how would the boy recognize the spot if Jim rushed? A mile from Cindy's car, Jim noticed disturbed gravel in the road. He knew cougars dragged their kills into cover. But he counseled himself not to jump to conclusions, and said nothing. Moments later, David pointed through the windshield.

"Right up here," he said.

David and Karen jumped out and ran up the road, yelling, "Mum!" and "Cindy!" Jim scanned the road and ditch bank. He saw horses' tracks in the road, spaced close, made by slow-moving animals. Then milling confusion. Then the hoofprints headed the opposite way, wide-spaced, at full gallop. The boy had found the spot, all right.

He was staring at those hoof marks when he heard a woman's voice. It said clearly, calmly, "Over here."

Cindy Parolin was alive. Jim realized he hadn't believed she would be. The voice came from the side of the road, near where David and Karen stood. He stared, but saw only willow thicket and shadow.

Suddenly uneasy, Jim called David and Karen back to the truck. Cindy was alive, but she wasn't strolling out onto the road. He asked Karen to turn the truck around and drive toward the voice. He, armed with the old shotgun, would walk.

Jim moved carefully. Cindy must be injured, and though hurrying might save her life, if the cat were still around, it could end his.

"Cindy, is the cat in the area?" he called.

Her voice came immediately, small but almost conversational: "Yes."

It had originated near the road, twenty paces ahead. He moved forward again, even more slowly.

There was no blood on the road, no sign of struggle in the brush or down the 4-foot ditchbank, only those scuffed bits of gravel he had noticed from the truck.

"Is the cat with you?"

"Yes."

Yes? It seemed unbelievable, but he couldn't doubt that voice. He was close enough to pinpoint it this time, a thick tangle of willow 20 feet in diameter just below the ditchbank in a grassy meadow. Jim tried to make his eyes push leaves and twigs aside, but all he saw was shadow. He stepped forward.

Then an electric tingle ran up his neck to his hairline: A new-looking riding jacket lay on the road bank, collar pointed toward him. It looked as though it had been carefully placed there.

This fit none of the scenarios Jim had been constructing. The kids had told him she was wearing her jacket when the cat attacked. He'd been glad to hear it, thinking the oilskin would protect her. If Cindy had been dragged to this point from the spot David had pointed out, 100 yards up the road, how did the jacket end up here, clean and neatly folded in half? For some reason, this unwieldy detail bothered him almost as much as the thought that a cougar might be crouched paces away.

Jim heard the truck pull up behind him.

"Cindy, is it right next to you?"

"Yes."

Jim drew back. He needed to think. His cow dog, Kala, had almost certainly dived back into the truck at the sight of the shotgun. That was good; she'd be safe there.

"Karen, put Trem in the truck," he yelled. The golden was young and not completely trained. It also wasn't his. When he heard the truck door slam, he turned his attention back to Cindy. What kind of reassurance would he want if he was her?

"Cindy, we have your kids," he said. "They're all OK."

Silence. He wished he could see her. He wished he could see the cat. When the voice came again, it was smaller still, but just as calm.

"I'm dying," it said.

Jim eased forward again, and this time he saw her. Her legs pointed toward him from 10 feet away, and they looked OK. He scanned up her body. Her clothing wasn't ripped or blood-soaked. Jim felt hope rising, despite Cindy's words and his own growing awareness that the air was saturated with the iron tang of blood. Then he leaned in from a slightly different angle and saw her head. That wasn't good. There was something, but it was hard to tell what in that green cave, badly wrong with her face.

What he saw next shocked him, even though he had believed Cindy's calm report. It was the cat. Its chest pressed against her right shoulder, its dark face low so its chin was immediately over hers. It stared at Jim. How had he had not seen those eyes?

The sight was almost a relief. Now Jim could forget the weird vision of that neatly arranged jacket, the woman's damaged face and her gentle admonition that she was out of time. He had to get that cat off Cindy Parolin. And he had to do it before daylight faded completely.

Jim knew cougars were strong and fast—this one had overpowered two people already—but he didn't think his mission was a difficult one. Unlike Cindy, he was armed. He raised the shotgun, then stopped: brush obscured most of the cat's body. The old Remington 12-gauge was loaded with light shot that, even at close range, could be deflected by twigs into Cindy's arm, shoulder, and face. Some rescuer he'd be if he killed the woman he'd come to save.

He needed the cat to move, to present a better target. He reached back, grabbed two fist-sized rocks, and threw them into the brush above the cat. It didn't twitch. It just beamed those huge eyes at him. The next rock hit the cougar in the neck hard enough that Jim heard the meaty thud. Still it didn't move.

He took another step forward and aimed the shotgun above the cat's head. The weapon crashed. Leaves and twigs rained onto the animal. Unbelievably, it remained a statue. Jim was beginning to get angry and very, very worried, but he was also fascinated. What kind of animal didn't flinch at the discharge of a firearm 4 feet away?

And more important, what now? Cindy hadn't spoken again. She needed help, and right now. He could feel David's eyes on his back. He was pretty sure the cat's eyes were still glued to him as well. But if he had to choose, he'd face the cat before he'd say to a thirteen-year-old boy, "I give up. I don't know what to do. Your mother will just have to die."

His last options, neither very attractive, were to use his brother-in-law's expensive young bird dog as bait, or throw himself at the cat. He'd start with the dog.

"Karen, let Trem out," he called.

Jim wasn't sure what to ask of the approaching dog. But it occurred to him that if Trem circled the thicket, the cat might rise for a better look or even give chase. Either way, Jim would get his shot.

"Circle, Trem," he said, for lack of a better command, and waved his arm vaguely as if the gesture should mean something to the young dog.

The golden stared at him a moment. Then, amazingly, he wheeled to trot a big circle around the willows, leaving Jim's right hand and returning to his left, exactly as Jim had envisioned. But the cougar didn't move, didn't even glance away from the man.

Now Jim noticed what looked like a rabbit run entering the

willows from behind. It led straight to the cat. Jim hated to sacrifice this obedient dog, but what choice remained?

"Circle, Trem," he said reluctantly, waving his arm as before. And the dog began again to trot around the willow thicket. When the flashes of yellow that were Trem reached the rabbit run, Jim tightened his grip on the shotgun, silently apologized to the dog, and yelled, "Get 'em!"

The dog wheeled into the tunnel and charged the cougar's back. But Jim never got a shot. The cougar spun so fast that Jim registered only blurred motion and then the cat was flying at Trem, screened by the tangled willows.

Trem was slightly smaller than the cougar. He was the color of chamois; the cat was brown with a darker stripe down its back. The force of the cat's attack somersaulted them up the rabbit tunnel and five or six times across the clearing, a silent gold and brown knot. When the tumbling stopped, Trem seemed surprised to find himself on top. The dog hesitated an instant, then leaped free and bolted for the road.

Jim heard Karen yell, "He's in the truck," but he didn't have time to be relieved for his brother-in-law's good dog. He was going to get his shot now, and he'd better not miss: with a smooth, boneless lope, the cat was coming straight for him.

Jim envisioned what would happen. As it approached, the cougar would leap a log that lay crosswise in the clearing 40 feet away. This would expose its chest and neck. Jim stood in a slight depression, just right of the thicket where Cindy lay. With his shotgun at his hip, the barrel would line up perfectly with the cat's exposed chest. That close, the old shotgun's pattern was 15 inches across. "I really can't miss," he told himself, and knew it to be true.

The cat didn't hesitate. It approached the log, and Jim reminded himself, "Squeeze, don't pull." Then it leaped, exactly as Jim had envisioned, and Jim contracted his forefinger.

Nothing happened.

"The gun's jammed!" he yelled at Karen. Previous experience

with the old weapon told him what had happened. The pump had slipped back a couple inches, preventing the firing mechanism from engaging. It would take a bare second to jack the pump, but in that second, his attention would be diverted from the approaching cat. Now that he'd seen how far a cougar could move in the blink of an eye, any inattention seemed foolish. He had always heard cougars were quick, but Jim Manion hadn't known that anything could move fast enough to literally blur.

Jim kept the useless gun aimed at the cat, mostly from habit, but he funneled all his energy into making his gaze a physical force. That cat had been staring at him nonstop. Fine. Two could play that game. Jim's grandfather had been a guide and a trapper. Maybe the old man had told him this would work. But whether from distant memory or gut instinct, he knew that if he stared hard enough, the cougar would stop before reaching him.

Ten feet away, it did. Eyes locked, man and cat stood motionless. A second stretched to ten, thirty, sixty.

Jim again considered snapping the gun up, jamming the pump and hoping the firing mechanism would engage. The trouble was, if it didn't, the cat would be on him.

He decided to back away. He'd do it smoothly, slowly. First he reached to his hip to unsnap his knife. The cat didn't seem to care what Jim did with his hand. Jim believed the cat cared very much what he did with his eyes, so he kept them locked forward even as he began to step back.

Jim's braces and thick-soled boots prevent his ankles from flexing. Nerve damage from the long-ago logging accident means Jim can't tell whether he's on flat ground or loose rock. Long practice has taught him to maintain balance by sensations in his knees, where he still has feeling. But that more distant checkpoint means Jim often can't know he's on unstable ground until after he begins to stumble.

As he backed into the 4-foot-high bank below the road, Jim remembered what it had looked like coming down: loose gravel, big rocks, and a little weedy vegetation. Jim was pretty sure a momentary loss of balance would bring the cat. So he allowed himself an instant as he placed each foot to dig with his heel, and listen for rock sounds. Then he committed his weight, grateful each time it held. The cat stepped forward a little more slowly than Jim retreated, as though their stares made an elastic but unbreakable band.

One last step and Jim's knees said he was on level ground. He'd made it to the road. Now he was able to move more quickly, gliding backward twenty feet or so to the truck and sidling behind the open driver's door, all before the cat appeared on the road.

Jim didn't realize until then that they had company. The cougar, as it followed Jim onto the road, faced a man, a woman, a boy, two dogs, a pickup truck, and now a blue van, from which a young man hopped, called "What's going on?" and saw the approaching cougar, jumped back into his vehicle, and slammed the door. Jim wasn't a cougar hunter, but he was born and raised in these parts, and he knew what everyone knew: cougars were shy, despite their formidable strength and speed. That this one, faced with such a crowd, merely stopped and stood in the road amazed him. It should have evaporated like a water droplet on a sun-struck rock.

After a few moments, though, the animal seemed ready to back down. It turned and began to walk away down the middle of the road, its stride slow and deliberate. Jim flashed angry. He jacked the pump and muttered to himself, "You're not getting away with this. I'm going to fill your butt with buckshot and you're going to know about hurt."

Aware he was not behaving rationally, he stepped from behind the door and strode after the cat. It wheeled around. Almost gleeful now, Jim aimed from the hip as he walked. That made round three, and Jim was tired of this game of eye war. Maybe the cougar was, too.

At 20 feet, Jim thought, the cat would drop and prepare to leap. When its chest touched the road, Jim would fire.

At 20 feet, the cat sank into a crouch. Jim squeezed the trigger.

This time the old shotgun roared. He saw fur ruffle on the animal's chest and heard pebbles skitter.

What happened next still awes him. From that short distance, Jim knew his shotgun would blow a hole through plywood. He expected the cat to be slung sideways by the impact. But for one frozen instant, it didn't even flinch. Then, as if the dirt road had become unbearably hot, the cougar uncoiled straight into the air. For a moment it seemed to hang, paws dangling 3 feet off the road. Then it dropped back, only to uncoil again in a sailing arc that took it perhaps 20 feet to the road's edge. Three more such leaps and it was gone.

Jim couldn't help thinking this was no normal cougar. Could it be normal for a cougar to crouch unflinching when a shotgun was discharged right over its head? To face four humans, two dogs, and two vehicles? To execute such amazing leaps when Jim knew he had badly wounded it? To attack a grown woman?

Karen was already crouched beside Cindy. She was yelling, "We're here, Cindy. We're people." Jim thought fast about that barely glimpsed face and called David. He was relieved when the boy came running toward the front of the truck instead of toward his mother. Good, obedient boy.

"Listen, do you know how to operate this?" he said, holding out his shotgun.

"Yes."

"Show me."

And the boy did. Jim glanced at the willow thicket and positioned David so he couldn't easily see inside.

"Stay here. And if the lion comes back, shoot it," ordered Jim.

"OK."

"You know your mother's been hurt very badly?"

"Yes."

"We're talking fifty-fifty here, David. Do you understand?"

The boy nodded. Jim told himself it wasn't a lie, that he wasn't sure she was dead.

Karen was still shouting into Cindy's face as Jim threaded into the thicket. The van driver was there, too. He seemed upset.

"Why are you doing that to her?" he said.

"I sure as hell don't want her to think I'm that cougar," she snapped. "I want her to know she won't be hurt anymore."

Jim smelled something faint and unpleasant. It tugged at an old memory he couldn't quite grab hold of.

Then he saw Cindy's face. He took in a staring eye and the bloody socket where the other eye had been. He saw a mouth so badly ripped it was hard to imagine it had spoken those clear words. Like her son, the woman had been partially scalped. Had the cougar done this while Jim stood up on the road, while Cindy spoke to him? The thought made him nearly sick with sympathy. Karen stopped yelling. Her look and a tiny shake of her head told him the rest.

Then the memory came: a bad car wreck when Jim was nineteen, a friend suddenly dead beside him, and a vague, putrid smell that Jim would later decide was the stinking signature of death itself. Karen had left the cabin barefoot, as usual. Jim would notice late that night that she was coated to the ankles in bloody mud, but the smell wasn't the smell of blood. It lay beneath that metallic sharpness like a shadow.

They decided quickly that the boy didn't need to know yet. They'd act as though Cindy was alive and send her body ahead in the van. Jim, Karen, and the children would follow in Jim's truck.

As the three carried their muddy, bloody load onto the road, Jim blocked David's view with his body, but the effort was unnecessary. The boy was doing as he'd been told. He was watching the forest edge. He didn't ask if he could ride with his mother, either. Maybe he saw through the charade. Maybe he was just too tired to question.

It was nearly dark by the time the van was headed toward Princeton. At 10:00 P.M. at Princeton General Hospital, where Cindy Parolin once worked, she was officially pronounced dead.

Jim turned his truck back toward the dusty brown Celica. They rounded up the two younger children and left a note for Les, the children's father. As he slid behind the wheel, Jim glanced at Karen. She held the little boy, Steven, in her lap, cradling his head in her right arm. Jim could see blood beginning to soak through the towels. Steven, David, and Melissa had been through so much. Jim felt as proud and protective of them as if they had been his own.

A few moments later, Melissa asked the question he had been dreading. "How bad is she?"

Jim couldn't answer. He silently begged David to have believed the lie, to repeat it now for Melissa.

"How bad is she?" Melissa asked again. Jim could hear tension in her voice. Silence stretched. They don't have to know this yet, Jim thought. They shouldn't hear this from strangers. We shouldn't have to tell them.

Finally, David spoke. "It's fifty-fifty, Melissa. She's hurt pretty bad. Right, Jim?"

Jim silently thanked the boy.

Late that night, with Steven safely in a hospital bed, Melissa and David were told another lie, one which they and their father believed for many years: Cindy Parolin died on the way to the hospital.

For a moment, standing in the waiting room, Melissa felt hot anger. Why did Mum have to save Steven? Why did she let it kill her? In the next moment, she remembered her mother telling an angry, crying brother a few months before, "I don't ever want to lose any of you." And she swelled with sudden pride. Her mother had meant it. She had died rather than lose a child.

Many were proud of Cindy Parolin. Canada posthumously awarded her a medal for civilian bravery, the Star of Courage. A display in Princeton's visitor center honors her. People as far away as Australia were moved to offer condolences after they read her story in their newspapers.

When Les Parolin went searching for his family that night, friends of the van driver told him his wife was dead. A cougar hunter himself, Les doesn't think one small cougar could kill a woman twice its size. He thinks two young cougars were traveling together when one noticed Steven. After Cindy sent the children away, the other emerged, attacking from behind. But no other cat was seen by witnesses or by officials who, later that night, followed a set of tracks to a dead cougar. Jim's old shotgun had done fatal damage after all.

However, Les is not the only person who has questions. At 63 pounds, this cougar was half the weight of its victim. Adults attacked by full-sized cougars have fought them off barehanded. Those who, like Cindy Parolin, attack cougars to rescue another nearly always walk away unscathed. Why is this woman dead? Stop a moment and think. Cindy had her riding jacket on when the children last saw her. When and why did she remove, fold, and lay it on the ground, especially if she was dragged to that spot? If she was badly injured when Melissa heard her scream, what happened in the long, long hour that followed, before the Manions and David returned?

It seems deeply unfair that nobody, not even the child whose life she saved, will ever know the shape of the price she paid for him.

14
Something Wrong at Cuyamaca

In this controversial newspaper photo, rangers Laura Itogawa and Earl Jones react after shooting an aggressive cougar in California's Cuyamaca Rancho State Park.

In most California state parks, cougar reports filed by rangers read like this: "Lion passing through wildlands," or "A camper reported that she saw a lion across the road," or "lion stood ground and watched people in campsite #4."

But in Cuyamaca Rancho State Park, a cluster of high, cool canyons right behind San Diego, the reports read more like a police blotter. Park visitors are "confronted by a lion," or "chased by a lion at close range." A ten-year-old girl is bitten, a three-year-old is rushed, bicyclists are threatened. There are twice as many cougar complaints from Cuyamaca as from any other California state park.

The cougars people complain about in Cuyamaca follow hikers, forcing them to back down the trail in herky-jerky stand-offs. Sometimes they make repeated rushes at small groups of people. They hiss or snarl, lay their ears back, and bare their teeth. Eventually, the people reach a car or a crowd. The cougars slowly turn and walk away.

It's been going on for more than a decade. Since 1987, game wardens responding to complaints have killed almost twenty cougars in Cuyamaca, many times more than any place else in the state. What adds urgency to the reports is that Cuyamaca is the only developed California park in which a cougar has killed a visitor.

"Cuyamaca" is what the Kumeyaay Indians called the place. It meant "the rain beyond." This mile-high park in the arid Peninsular Range is 3 miles wide and 10 miles long and contains green glens unlike anything else in that part of Southern California. For up to two weeks after a winter storm, the oak and pine forests hold snow, beckoning sunburnt San Diegans. The park draws almost a half-million people some years.

You can see San Diego from the 6,500-foot summit of Cuyamaca Peak, but safety signs warn visitors they're on the home ground of a predator. "Lions at Cuyamaca have been known to be unusually aggressive," park maps say.

State wildlife experts estimate there are probably no more than a dozen cougars whose home ranges include the park at any given time. Since guns are forbidden, visitors who wish to protect themselves are encouraged to carry sticks and rocks, which rangers find in little piles at the park's trailheads. The region's merchants sometimes complain that the park scares away business by overstating the risk, but some park visitors and even local game wardens say the opposite. They gripe that the rangers are so focused on wildlife preservation they don't take the confrontations seriously enough.

Indeed, the cougar problem has gotten worse, not better. When supervising ranger Lt. Laura Itogawa was assigned to Cuyamaca in 1988, the staff told her a few cougar stories, but shrugged them off as flukes. One cougar had been shot by a Fish and Game lieutenant named Bob Turner after it holed up in the nearby scout camp's ceremonial teepee. It turned out to have bubonic plague. Other cougars had rushed or followed people. Like her staff, Laura dismissed the stories, since there were no confrontations during her first five years at the park. Her attitude toward cougars was just like that of most rangers: visitors who got to see one were lucky.

Laura had all but grown up in the ranger service. A native of the San Diego suburbs, she turned her love of deserts and mountains into a job leading overnight hiking trips, then became a seasonal ranger. She left college at 19 to work full time for California State Parks.

Laura is 5 foot 1 inch, 110 pounds, fit, and forceful, a woman who has spent her career outdoors in lug-soled boots and green jeans with a pistol on her hip. But a ranger's gun is for controlling humans, not for killing animals, she says. Or at least she used to.

Game agencies nationwide are divided along caricatured lines: redneck game wardens vs. bunny hugger biologists and rangers. Laura didn't like it, but the wardens and rangers around Cuyamaca had faced off in the same way. Bob Turner groused that rangers hid cougar complaints from him and his staff. Rangers said Bob and the wardens who worked for him were cowboys, too quick to shoot. Laura had quickly figured out that Bob was plenty smart about the park and loved wildlife in his own way. His intolerant redneck act was his way of mocking the assumptions rangers and others made about wardens. If they were too quick to judge, it was their loss; they'd never get the benefit of his knowledge.

In June of 1993, a lion stalked a young family on the Azalea Glen Trail in the heart of the park. The man and his wife had one child in a backpack, the other firmly in hand. The lion batted at the man's six-foot stick as the family backed all the way to camp. The next day, Bob Turner tracked it down and shot it.

Laura talked over the Azalea Glen incident with her boss, the park superintendent, and increased the number of warning signs, but it didn't seem like enough. A cougar like that was more aggressive than any she had heard of in other California parks. Plus, it sounded like the cougar stories she had dismissed when she arrived at Cuyamaca. You could second-guess Bob's decision to kill it, but she had read about maulings in British Columbia and couldn't imagine what she'd say to a parent if a child were hurt by an aberrant cougar the park had tolerated.

Laura met with biologists, wardens, and rangers and then wrote new cougar rules for Cuyamaca. From now on, visitors would be cleared out of the park after worrisome incidents. Bold cats would be killed, particularly those that approached people in broad daylight. Laura didn't much like the sound of the new rules, but she took comfort in the thought that removal of aggressive cougars would make it safer for people to live with the rest.

That September a lion chased a couple on horseback for more than a quarter mile down the Stonewall Creek fire break. The riders had reined their horses when they spotted the lion along the trail. It didn't run away. It turned and approached them. Spooked, they galloped away down the trail, but the cougar chased them. This lion had broken the new rule.

Laura and her boss decided to close the park for two weeks, the biologists' best guess of the longest a cougar might hang around if it had a deer carcass cached nearby. She called in the federal hunters from Animal Damage Control, an agency of the U.S. Department of Agriculture. Expecting tobacco-chewing good old boys, she was pleased to find the team carefully professional about their work. They conducted a thorough but unsuccessful search for the cat.

People called to complain about the hunt. Aren't rangers supposed to keep hunters out of the parks? When the federal hunters said they thought the cat had moved on, her boss decided to open the park a day early.

On reopening day, campers were jumpy and cat-happy. With a *Los Angeles Times* reporter and photographer tagging along, Laura headed out to check the first report: a camper had seen a cougar crossing a road. She was interrupted by her radio en route. A cougar had just sauntered through a 120-person group camp, circling tents and sniffing the butt of a woman bent over tying her shoe. Laura hurried to the group camp and was looking for tracks when the radio hissed again: A cougar had mauled a dog at the other end of the group camp. Laura gunned her car the quarter mile down the road.

A man and his son were waving their arms as she pulled in. Their tiny dog was alive, but lying still with its shoulder torn open. The cougar went up there, the man said, pointing up a nearby fire road.

Laura took several deep breaths and let them out slowly as she slid the pole gate out of the way. This cat would have to be killed, she realized, and there wasn't time to call for help. She had shot deer found thrashing in the ditch after a car hit them, but that was mercy. This was going to be more like what game wardens and federal hunters did.

"537? 225," she called into the radio. She was rolling quietly up the fire road on a thick mat of pine needles and spongy forest duff, looking into the trees on either side. "225, go ahead," her boss, Greg Picard, came back right away.

"We've got a lion that mauled a dog and they say it's right ahead of me on the road and it's been in the full campground," she told him. "I believe it's a take."

"According to the protocol, I concur," Picard said. "It's a take."

A patch of sunshine 25 feet away caught her eye.

"Oop! There he is now!" she told Picard, and signed off. The cougar stood in the little clearing with his ears pricked. He looked playful to her and much smaller than the lion described by the riders who were chased two weeks before. She heard the reporters pull in behind her, followed by Earl Jones, a ranger who had trained with her in the 1970s and now worked for her.

She and Jones each jacked a shell into place and spread out. They shouldered their shotguns, aimed and fired. When she refocused after the recoil, the cougar was gone. She looked at Jones. "Where did it go?"

"Up the draw," he said, pointing with his chin.

They climbed slightly rising ground in the sun-dappled brush under tall oaks. Almost immediately she saw the cougar, lying under a manzanita bush 20 feet away, flicking its tail. "There he is," she called to Earl as she leveled her shotgun and fired.

"He's still alive, shoot him again," she said. Jones did, and the cougar stopped moving.

Relief and regret overwhelmed her. Jones, who stands better than 6 feet tall and is slim the way Laura is, was rubbing his temples. The photographer's camera clicked away.

"We need a private moment," Jones said, raising a hand toward the lens. The camera stopped.

"I need a hug," he said to Laura and she wrapped her arms around him. When they stepped back, Jones, a little below Laura, was holding his face in one hand, shotgun in the other, while Laura stood grimacing at the sky. The shutter clicked.

"It's done," she told Picard back at her car. She would later learn that, in the confused moments before the cougar attacked the dog, it had also bitten a little girl. The footprints of the dead cat matched plaster casts of the lion that chased the riders two weeks before.

The next morning, Laura and Earl crying over the dead cat was on the front page of the *Los Angeles Times.* Hate mail and phone calls began pouring in.

"You tell officer Jones and officer Itogawa they're going to hell and I'm going to pray for them to go to hell," a caller said. When a game warden like Bob Turner shoots a cat, the calls all go to the regional Fish and Game office down in San Diego, not to the warden himself. But these calls and letters came straight to park headquarters. Laura and Earl caught the full force. One cryptic critic pasted the photo from the *Times* onto the lower body of a woman from a pornographic magazine and mailed it to Laura.

Laura felt like she was taking it from all sides. Some state park

*California game warden Bob Turner has killed many of
Cuyamaca Rancho State Park's most aggressive cougars.*

rangers, steeped in the idea that their job is to save wildlife and
wildlands from the public, were just as furious as the callers. Then
there were old-timers who thought it was a good idea to kill the
cat, but not to cry about it, especially in front of a news photographer. Game wardens like Bob thought it was a little silly to cry,
but they could relate to Laura's situation. Everyone's a critic when
you're making judgment calls about safety and wildlife, Bob said.
He was glad to see a ranger take care of some of the park's dirty
work. Laura hunkered down and waited. Critics and cougars quieted down for a year.

In May of 1994, however, a three-year-old boy was rushed on
the Azalea Glen Trail by a cougar that bared its teeth and
crouched low before the boy's father drove it away with a stick.
The cat was hunted down and killed. So was the next cougar to
threaten a visitor that year.

Laura believed the biting of the little girl in the group camp
had at least convinced all the rangers that bold cats could become

a serious risk. But there was still a big difference between the rangers, who were inclined to give cougars the benefit of the doubt, and Bob Turner and the game wardens, who were not. Laura felt her sympathies divided.

She was meeting with the park's volunteer corps upstairs in the historic stone headquarters on December 10, when a ranger barked her call number over the radio. Two hikers had just shown up with a backpack, a knit cap, a pair of women's glasses, and a tooth. They'd found the items near a puddle of blood on the fire road up Cuyamaca Peak.

Minutes later, one of the hikers, an off-duty California Highway Patrolwoman, handed Laura a blue daypack slimy with what felt like saliva. The rangers Laura had sent to check the scene radioed in to say they were on-site and could see something blue off in the bushes.

"Proceed single file with your guns drawn," Laura told them.

"We've got an 11-44," the ranger radioed back. That meant a dead body on the ground. Laura drove up the steep fire road, thinking, "What do I want, an axe murderer or a lion? An axe-murderer," she told herself.

Laura, her rangers, and a San Diego County deputy walked single file through the brush. The dead woman's blue sweatpants were bunched at her ankles. She was mostly naked and there were too many puncture wounds in her back to count. But as Laura stared, the picture came into focus. The sweatpants hadn't been yanked down; they were snagged on a tree limb. The punctures weren't stab wounds. They came in sets of four. Her scalp had been peeled off, starting at the nape. Damn. No human did this.

The longer she stood over the body, the sadder she became. The woman had been dragged by her head to the dark spot in the woods. But she must have been alive when she got there because her arms were not trailing along, they were pulled up to cradle her head. Judging by the smears on the woman's right arm, she had mopped the blood from her forehead before she died. The smears were still bright and wet. She had probably been alive ten minutes ago.

The sheriff's deputy, convinced the victim had been murdered, hung crime scene tape. Laura was sure he was wrong. The bite wounds could only have been the work of a cougar. But the scene couldn't be disturbed nor the cougar hunted until police investigators agreed. Dispatch said the detectives' arrival would depend on how many murders there had been in San Diego that day. It was 11:30 A.M. She asked dispatch to call Bob Turner. This cougar had to die.

They were unlikely friends, but she'd learned to trust him. He's a classic macho game warden. Born of California pioneer stock, he grew up hiking, like Laura. But when he was on foot, he was hunting deer, usually in the foothills north and south of the park. Like Laura, he also started out as a ranger, patrolling citified parks where scuffles with what he calls "human trash" were common. He keeps himself fit, wears a thick mustache, and drives a big truck. Bob arms himself with a pistol, a steady stream of politically incorrect jokes, a firm grasp of field biology, and a zoology degree on which Laura had come to depend.

It was Bob's day off, but when he heard "They think someone's been killed by a lion," he jumped in his truck and sped the fifteen minutes to the park.

"This one can't get away," he thought. If you don't catch a goat-killing cougar, it may return to kill another goat. But a man killer? The rangers could talk all they wanted about how bold cougars were just curious and could be safely left alone. And the public could fire off as much hate mail as it pleased. This one Bob had to find.

The deputy wouldn't let Bob near the body. Homicide still hadn't arrived with their tweezers and plastic baggies. Bob listened to Laura and agreed this was probably a cougar kill. But he couldn't be sure until he saw for himself, and he couldn't turn the hounds loose until the detectives said OK.

"Let me tell you something, people," he told the small crew bundled against the wind. "If this is a lion, the fact that he killed

Photo courtesy of Kathleen Seefeldt

Iris Kenna, a high school counselor and avid birdwatcher, was killed by a cougar on Cuyamaca Peak in December 1994.

somebody shows that he's not afraid of us. So keep your eyes open and don't be surprised if we see him peeking around a rock or over a log at us."

There was nothing boring about the wait. The adrenaline made them all have to pee, but no one wanted to squat in the woods alone, so they trooped out in pairs, one doing his or her business, the other standing guard.

Laura got more spooked as the daylight faded. She still didn't know the victim's name, but spending the day 15 feet from her, she began to feel she knew her. They wore the same cheap Timex outdoor watch. They both had sun wrinkles around their eyes.

Later, Laura would learn that the victim was a birdwatcher, like many of Laura's friends. Iris Kenna, fifty-six, had been a guidance counselor at an alternative high school in San Diego. The job gave her plenty of time to load up her Toyota pickup and drive the west coast or the desert southwest to go birding.

As Laura waited, she had the strong sense that the cat was out there, just like Bob said.

"You know what? I'm feeling really weird," Laura told the big beefy deputy she had assigned to stand guard over the crime scene with her.

"I am too," the big guy said, looking around.

It was almost dark when the homicide detective arrived, straight off the streets of San Diego in an expensive wool overcoat, a suit, and shiny dress shoes. Bob and Laura stopped him on the pavement of the Cuyamaca Peak road. "I can really help you guys out here if you just let me look at the body," Bob said, explaining that Laura thought the wounds matched cougar bite marks. The detective let him into the crime scene.

Bob was instantly certain. All over the woman's back and shoulders were tooth punctures in a characteristic box pattern. The 12-inch gaping rip under her left arm looked like the work of that huge thumb claw.

Bob was horrified. The woman had survived the first leaping tackle, even though her head hit the ground hard enough to knock out a tooth. She even fought back a little. From what he could tell, she may have been alive when the cougar began chewing a patch of her scalp. It made him duck his head and cringe in sympathy. It's hard enough to shake a five-pound housecat from your arm if it wants to hurt you. This was a wild cat more than twenty times heavier, with five huge fishhooks on every paw and four dagger-like canine teeth in a bone-cracking jaw. What else could this lone hiker have done once she was stunned and on the ground but wait for it to finish her off?

Iris's body was bagged for removal, and Bob moved in. A hound hunter's radio dog collar was strapped to a nearby sapling. The removable magnetic "on" switch was tied to a deer Bob had shot to fool the cougar when it returned. If the deer was moved, the radio collar would sound.

Back down the mountain, Bob and a small group of federal hunters and rangers packed their gear and checked guns and flashlights. They were speculating how long they would wait when one of the federal hunters realized he hadn't turned on the receiver yet. When he did, the radio collar was already sounding. It had been just twenty minutes since they left the scene.

Back on Cuyamaca Peak, Bob was nervous. The lion must have been just out of sight all day; it must have watched them leave. The deer carcass was gone, but there were no drag marks. This lion was big enough to pick up an adult doe and carry her.

The hounds were barking from the back of the truck like they'd already struck scent. Released, they headed south, baying the distinctive bark that says the scent is fresh. The lion contoured along the ridge for a half mile before it treed. When Bob arrived, he trained his flashlight upward.

"Holy shit!" he thought. All of the problem cougars he'd seen in Cuyamaca were juveniles, 60, 70, and 80 pounds. He thought of them as troubled teenagers. This was a huge male, 130 pounds from the look of him. "Now we've got adult males attacking us?" he thought. "We don't stand a chance."

Laura hadn't slept well all night after she got the call that the cougar was dead. The next morning, she ducked into the park's maintenance shop to look at the dead cougar. "Look what you've done," she thought, knowing cougar hunting advocates would use this as evidence for their cause. "Look what you've done to your friends."

In the years after Iris's death, Iris's birdwatcher friends would criticize the killing of the cougar, saying it was only behaving naturally and that Iris would have wanted to die in the way she did, getting woven back into the web of life as food for a wild animal.

Easy to say if you didn't see the excruciating wounds, say Laura and Bob. They both snort at the idea that anybody would choose the lonely agony so obvious to them that night on Cuyamaca Peak. Bob began to notice the hair standing on the back of his neck whenever his work took him to the windy summit. He hurried to get away from the memories. Laura backpacks alone into the Sierra Nevada and the deserts of Arizona, sharing terrain with cougars and bears. But she stopped walking her own park's trails alone. She won't make her rangers do it, either. On the rare occasions she has to move through the park's backcountry alone, she carries a heavy stick slung across her shoulders to protect her neck and she has learned to spin constantly, keeping track of what's behind her.

For a year after Iris's death, there were no serious cougar problems. But in January of 1996, a woman had to charge her horse at a cougar that confronted her. Bob shot it the next day as it charged another game warden. Laura began to think there was some genetic quirk in the park's cats that made them more aggressive.

In September of 1998, Bob and another warden killed four cougars in two days, all near a horse camp in the park, after campers reported a series of stalkings and charges. Shawn Pirtle, the first game warden on the scene, was amazed when a ranger suggested, even after all the disturbing complaints, that they only shoot cougars that failed to run away.

Even though those four cats were probably siblings, Bob is convinced it isn't genetics so much as environment that makes some Cuyamaca cougars dangerous. He deals with cougars all over San Diego County, but only sees aggressive cats in Cuyamaca, where a steady stream of people flood the lions' habitat. Cats that see people from their first day out of the womb don't fear them and are more likely to consider them a food source, he says.

By 1999, the state of California had decided to take Bob, Laura, and the Cuyamaca cougar problem seriously. That year, the legislature approved $200,000 for a study in Cuyamaca. Within a year, that money had attracted additional funding and the scope of the project grew. California voters, an anomymous donor, and the U.S. Fish and Wildlife Service committed another $375,000, enough to fund a ten-year study of mountain lions, mule deer, and desert bighorn sheep in the region. Hornocker researchers Linda Sweanor and Kenny Logan will lead the lion capture portion of the study.

Meanwhile, piles of rocks and sticks continue to accumulate at the park's trailheads.

14
Lightning Strikes Twice

Trail runners Diane Shields and Lucy Oberlin have learned more than they wanted to know about aggressive cougars in Cuyamaca Rancho State Park.

Photo courtesy of Lucy Oberlin

"Why are you getting out of the car?" Diane asked nervously.

"I want to see if I can stand," said Lucy Oberlin. A uniformed employee talked to the car ahead over a Cuyamaca Rancho State Park map. Lucy found herself waiting politely until the woman glanced back.

"I want to report a mountain lion attack," she said, startled by how hoarse she sounded.

"Oh, did you just see one, dear?"

"No, we just had a twenty-minute fight with one."

The woman stared for a moment before replying, "Well, you don't look injured."

"I want to make a report," Lucy croaked stubbornly.

The woman looked more closely, and then her voice became briskly professional. "Let me call a ranger to talk to you, OK?"

Lucy and Diane told their story to the heavy-set ranger who arrived a few minutes later. He took careful notes, but he also said things that made Lucy uncomfortable. He suggested they not repeat their story to the media. He told them park rangers receive death threats every time "one of these things happens." He joked that the lion exhibited good taste in singling out these two women. He seemed to think Lucy and Diane were overreacting, that they might make people think mountain lions were dangerous.

"But they *are* dangerous," Lucy thought. This was 1997: it was common knowledge that weird cougar encounters occurred in this park. A woman had been killed a few years back, a child bitten. And today, she and Diane might have died. Something should be done. She wasn't thinking well enough yet to have an idea what, but clearly this man in front of her was one of the people who ought to do it.

Lucy had run the trails in Cuyamaca for seventeen years. When she lived in San Diego, she made the hour-long drive once a week. For the last five years she'd lived a few minutes from Cuyamaca on I-8, in a little town called Alpine. This allowed her to run and walk the park's oak-forested hills nearly every other day.

Often she ran with Diane Shields, her partner in a cookie dough company called "Your Mama's Cookies." Lucy is forty. Her passion for running weathers her skin brown between the freckles. Her hair is dyed blond, and then sun-bleached to an uncompromising near-white. Lucy and Diane have been friends for nearly two decades.

Lucy talks in emotional hyperbole. If she was frightened, she describes queasy, knee-quivering terror. If she was sad, she bawled for an hour, couldn't eat, couldn't sleep. But you get the impression, studying her ramrod carriage and direct gaze, that she's never met a problem too big, after the emoting, to beat.

On this baking August day in 1997, the two had taken Lucy's gray minivan to Cuyamaca's Cold Stream trailhead. Their route would provide a pretty view from the summit of Stonewall Peak and a 14-mile out-and-back run. At about 1:00 P.M., they strapped on fanny packs and water bottles. Each grabbed a slim black canister of pepper spray.

The women had started carrying pepper spray years before after encountering perhaps thirty armed men on a Cuyamaca trail. The men had broken out in excited yells and chased them. When the women gained a little distance, they ducked into thick brush. The men ran past, yelling, "chicas," and "Andale!" and other words the runners didn't understand. Encounters with what locals call "illegals" are not uncommon in Cuyamaca and surrounding areas. The Mexican border is barely a day's determined walk south.

On this day, the incident grown vague in their minds, the two carried the canisters mostly from habit. They ran north on Cold Stream Trail, Lucy leading as usual. They intersected the Stonewall Peak Trail, which took them to the top of the mountain. From the summit, the women could see desert stretching east from the mountains like ocean from an island. On a clear day, they would have glimpsed the Pacific, but haze to the west blocked that thin blue line. The women ran another half hour past the peak before turning back. About a mile before Cold Stream Trail would deliver them to the van, they began walking to cool down. Diane was talking excitedly to Lucy's back about something important that neither can now recall, so Lucy saw the mountain lion first.

It stood in the trail about 30 feet away. It stared at the women. Cuyamaca's oddly aggressive lions get a lot of press, so Lucy's response was fast and smart.

"Diane, there's a mountain lion. Start screaming."

"What what?" Diane replied lightly.

"Diane! Mountain lion. Start screaming."

As though spurred by Lucy's yell, the lion began trotting toward them. The movement drew Diane's eyes. Now she got it. Both women screamed hard and waved their arms. The lion neither slowed nor hastened. It isn't going to stop, Lucy thought. She extended the pepper spray before her. This is not supposed to happen. We yell and stand our ground and act big and it stops, but it isn't stopping.

Frantic, Lucy punched the button. A thin brown stream of fluid, about as wide as a pencil lead, extended from the little canister. It reached six feet—several feet short of the lion.

The big animal stopped, pulled its head back, and sniffed. Then, although its stare didn't waver, it backed up the embankment left of the trail and dropped into a half-crouch.

Lucy felt naked in the middle of the trail. A nearby cluster of five or six slim-trunked trees laced with brush offered at least the illusion of protection. Still yelling, she drew Diane up the slope, and the two pressed close to the trees.

Lucy felt something bang against her left arm. "Take it," Diane yelled. Lucy's free hand closed around a 5-foot-long stick.

The lion came then, fast and low. Lucy thrashed the brush with her stick. Diane threw rocks. The cat stopped just out of spray range, then backed up, eyes still on the women. "I'm covering you. Pick up more rocks," Lucy ordered.

"I'm scared. I can't."

"You have to. I'm covering you. Please, you have to."

Diane bent to the ground.

And so it went, for what Lucy guesses was fifteen minutes. The lion would stare, silent and intent, muscles bunched beneath the tan hide. Then it would drop low and rush them with ground-hugging grace. The women yelled at the lion to leave them alone, yelled for help. When they had something to say to each other, they yelled it. They banged their sticks and threw the rocks that Diane found at her feet. Despite all their noise, the lion came a little closer each time before it stopped, then backed up, still staring. Its ears would rise to the sulky, dangerous half-mast position that every housecat owner knows. Then the ears would again slick down to the round skull, and it would swarm toward the yelling, stick-banging women. Then withdrawal, then rush, then withdrawal, all in silence.

Lucy was sure she and Diane would escape—she would kill the lion if she had to—but when she tried to imagine how, her imagination painted pictures in blood. With each image, she became more terrified. This is really going to hurt, she thought.

The standoff was taking a greater toll on Diane. At one point she screamed out, "This has got to stop. We've got to get out of here."

"We can't run, Diane. We have to get out of here alive."

Moments later, she glanced back to see Diane rocking rhythmically forward and back, white-faced, eyes half-lidded and vague. Lucy grabbed her arm, squeezed as hard as she could and yelled in her face, "Stay with me. You've got to stay with me."

Once more the lion rushed in, but this time it didn't stop. When it reached the far side of the little thicket, Lucy frantically thumbed her pepper spray, discharging the last of the thin stream directly into the left side of the cat's head and neck. Bullseye! The cat reared violently away, front paws scrubbing at the air, almost toppling over backward. This time Lucy imagined for a moment that it was leaving, but it only retreated a little farther from the trail, climbed onto a low boulder, and crouched, still staring.

The women were hoarse from shouting and lightheaded from fear. Neither doubted that they were fighting for their lives; neither believed, as they had at first, that the cat might tire of these noisy, rock-throwing humans and simply leave. Diane, pale and shaking, held the precious final canister of pepper spray.

Something had to change. Lucy eyeballed a heavy-trunked tree 4 feet from their current, precarious refuge, 4 feet closer to the parking lot and the van. The first few times they tried for it, the lion dropped from its boulder and rushed. Its rushes now were only feints of a few yards, but they were enough to drive the women back. On the seventh try, the lion allowed them to reach the tree. So they picked another. The animal didn't move as they slipped across the gap. They picked a third tree. Six trees later, they reached a bend in the trail that would face them straight at the road, still nearly a mile away.

Lucy and Diane hesitated, then slipped onto the trail and around the corner. Lucy was relieved to be finally doing something. But not seeing the lion was almost worse than watching its charges, so the two walked quickly, shoulder to shoulder and sometimes back to back, eyes straining into the heavy scrub oak and manzanita. Was it still on its boulder behind them, or was it ahead, crouched in the underbrush beside the trail?

When they could see the highway paralleling the trail through the trees, they cut through a steep gully to intersect it. They walked down the middle of the road a quarter mile to Lucy's car. Lucy dropped her stick at the car door, but she had to help Diane pry cramped fingers from around hers, revealing bloody half-moons on her palm. They got into the van and, each feeling the silliness of it, reached out to lock the doors.

Lucy's voice rasped in her throat for two months. She believes she is alive because neither woman panicked, because that particular day they had been running together, and because they carried pepper spray.

Lucy's report was one of several that led to the killing of four aggressive Cuyamaca lions. If she thought that was the end of it, though, she was wrong. When they read about the dead lions in the paper, Lucy's friends told her she shouldn't have reported the incident.

"I believe he would have killed someone," she told them, but her friends seemed not to hear. They talked about how beautiful lions are, how naturally curious they are, like housecats at play. With a confidence she recollects with thin-lipped anger, her friends assured her that the lion had never intended her harm.

Some were less kind. The park is known cougar habitat, they'd say. Strange cougar stories were common, so it wasn't like Lucy didn't know the risk. Yet she and Diane ran there anyway. The encounter was the women's fault, yet it was cougars, as usual, that paid the price.

One day, weeks after the encounter, a woman Lucy didn't know marched up to her in the grocery store. "You're the woman who killed four mountain lions, aren't you? You did kill them, you know."

The criticism made her cry, but it didn't stop her from running. Her solution? She purchased a .380 to carry in her fanny pack.

Guns are illegal in Cuyamaca Rancho State Park. That and Lucy's hippie upbringing in mellow Carmel, California made her uneasy about the lethal weight of the thing against her body. But Lucy couldn't imagine not running. She felt that those hours on Cuyamaca's forested trails made her a better, stronger person. She also couldn't imagine running without more serious protection than a finger-sized can of pepper spray. She wore a seatbelt when she drove a car, and she would now carry a gun in lion country.

This was not the hysterical victim who had expected the rangers to make her safe. Perhaps she had internalized some of the criticism of those first, tearful weeks after the encounter. Lucy still believed that running in the park was her right, but maybe that right had to be earned. Not by killing—she didn't ever expect to actually pull the little gun's trigger—but by being able to defend herself. Being ready.

For nearly a year the women avoided the area around Cold Stream Trail with superstitious distaste. Then one warm afternoon the next April, as they trained for a 38-mile race to be held that fall in Yosemite, they decided to run Eastside Trail, an old favorite. The trail would cross Cold Stream Trail about seven miles in.

Early in the run as they forded the Sweetwater River, they passed Cuyamaca Outdoor School, a camp that many San Diego County sixth-graders attend, and saw a dozen kids, sweatshirts knotted about their waists, teetering across the shallow river on boulders and logs. A single adult walked several yards ahead. Two kids straggled 10 yards behind. The empty air between those two and the rest made Lucy nervous. She promised herself that when her kids, aged eight and ten, came to the school, she'd go too, to bring up the rear on hikes.

Lucy no longer believed she could have killed, bare-handed, the cat that charged her and Diane. She had since seen police photos of two women killed by mountain lions, and the victims' devastating wounds stole her illusions. The lion had been in control that day on Cold Stream Trail. Lucy and Diane left unharmed because it let them leave. By what margin, for what reason, she could never know. She thought about the gun, stored in Diane's fanny pack, and, as usual, felt steadier.

On their return, the women again crossed the Sweetwater River, here only a narrow trickle, and sat on a cool, damp sandbar to stretch. They decided they felt more comfortable returning to Cold Stream Trail than they had expected. They reminded each other how slim, even in strange Cuyamaca, were the odds that they'd ever again face a mountain lion.

On the way down, a soft carpet of pine needles made running pleasant. Soon they were back at the camp, which this time they passed directly through. At the river bench, about fifty kids played tetherball, volleyball, badminton, and basketball. No adults were in sight. Then a bell rang from the camp buildings above. Half of the kids broke away and headed uphill. They must eat in shifts, Lucy thought. All the adults must be up there making dinner happen.

The women dropped to the little river, crossed on the same logs and rocks they'd seen the youthful hikers use, and zigzagged up a sandy trail on the far side. The trail hugged the lip of the steep bank, 15 feet above the water. The Sweetwater River here ran knee-deep and quiet over rocks and strips of sand. The far bank rose steeply as well.

Again, Lucy saw the lion first. It was across the river, thank God, on the far bank. An utterly irrational thought slipped into her head: If I don't look, it'll go away, or never have been there, or turn into a deer.

She turned her eyes resolutely to the trail ahead. Seconds passed, fifteen, twenty, thirty. Then she couldn't stand it. Her eyes darted left. The lion had not, of course, turned into a deer. It now glided parallel to the women, matching their speed, its body pointed downriver, its small head swiveled toward them.

"Diane? Get out the gun."

The animal was lovely, with a pale face, creamy soft-looking fur, and a long, thick tail, carried high. It seemed much larger than the other one. But although huge and heavy, it moved with a weightless grace that made Lucy feel clumsy. It seemed to float above the ground. Tall grasses brushed its belly.

Less than a quarter mile beyond the river, Lucy could see busy Highway 79 through the trees. What good was the gun here? Diane couldn't fire even if she wanted to. Who knew how far a bad shot might travel? Besides, this cougar was only shadowing them. Staring. Did that mean it would attack? Did that mean it wouldn't? Lucy found herself thinking nothing could stare as hard as a lion.

"Take it, take the gun. I can't get a bullet in the chamber."

Diane's tremulous voice alarmed Lucy. She looked back to see her friend extending the gun, barrel down, with a violently shaking arm. An instant later, Diane turned even whiter and stumbled to the ground. Lucy caught the gun by reflex. The lion spun and sank into a crouch. Suddenly all that was visible were its face and wide, intent eyes. This was not good. This was too much like a year ago. She yanked her friend to her feet. As soon as the women were walking again, the lion also rose and resumed its gliding accompaniment. Détente.

Lucy worked the slide and heard a cartridge click into the chamber. The .380 was ready to fire. "Don't shoot," Diane said. "There's cars out there."

"I won't. Not unless he comes to the river."

How fast could a mountain lion cover a narrow ribbon of shallow water and 15 feet of shore? Before she could shoot twice?

Once? Lucy had never practiced on a moving target. She felt queasy. For more than a mile, the lion shadowed the women. Lucy became more and more certain that it would not turn and charge, but she couldn't relax. That it followed them at all was deeply unnerving. If lions didn't fear people, what protection was there from a 100-pound animal that had practiced killing nearly from birth?

They caught their last glimpse of the lion when the trail curved away from the river into heavy brush. It was still staring, but it made no move to cross the river and follow. Two minutes later, they turned the last corner before the parking area and saw a young couple strolling ahead of them. The woman wore a white tube top and clear, platform jellies. She was tiny, the bones in her shoulders and arms readily visible beneath pale skin. They looked like city folk, a distinction Cuyamaca's locals were quick to make once they themselves no longer were.

"Are you headed to your car?" Lucy called from fifteen feet behind.

"Why?"

"*Because* we've been followed by a mountain lion for the past mile."

"Oh goody," the woman said. "I'd love to see a mountain lion. Let's go look for it. Where did you see it? When?"

"Unless you're carrying a gun or pepper spray, I don't think you want to do that." Lucy didn't hide her disgust. She still clutched the .380, although she tried to conceal it against her body.

The man looked at Lucy and back at his companion. Lucy thought perhaps he saw the gun.

"No. We're headed to our car," he said quickly.

Lucy and Diane brushed past them into the parking lot. Her stomach felt full of something. Fear? Relief? Whatever it was, she heaved it up onto the ground behind the bumper without embarrassment. Several minutes passed before she was willing to unload the .380 and put it in the trunk. Without it, the short walk to the driver's door stripped her naked.

"I'm sorry. I can't drive yet," she mumbled, beginning to be ashamed. Don't look and it'll disappear? How stupidly she had used that first, potentially critical moment.

"It was a beautiful lion," Diane said. As usual, once the crisis was past, she was rock steady. Lucy, who'd felt solid when the moments strung together like a tight wire over empty space, thought she might shake to pieces now.

"Beautiful? How can you say that?" she snapped.

"Lucy, it didn't get us. We're OK."

Lucy took a deep breath. Diane was right. "We're OK," she agreed.

And she remembered that she had also thought it beautiful.

Nevertheless, Lucy called in a report that night. Over the next few days, park staffers walked her through the encounter. Most seemed unsympathetic, maybe even doubtful. One woman Lucy took to be a ranger said that she herself had once viewed a lion and kitten, a lovely sight. When the woman added that she'd been sitting in a car at the time, Lucy was disgusted.

One ranger, a woman named Laura Itogawa, sounded more sympathetic. She asked Lucy to understand that the park stood in an awkward place, sworn to protect its wild inhabitants as well as its human visitors. This ranger assured Lucy that the cougar she described was not behaving in a way the park considered normal or safe, and that park staff did, indeed, have concerns about Cuyamaca's lions.

Lucy called Fish and Game's Bob Turner, unsure what she wanted, perhaps just someone to take her seriously. Bob suggested the cat might have been using the women to hunt, watching to see if they would flush deer. Lucy didn't buy it. She thought Bob was trying to make her feel better by making the lion's behavior seem less threatening. It didn't seem strange to her that a lion might let humans flush prey, but with its camouflage coloring and boneless grace, the animal could have stayed out of sight if it wished. Instead, it had allowed the women to know it was matching them, step for step. Why?

Lucy still runs in Cuyamaca Rancho State Park, but she no longer allows her children to hike there. After the second incident, she finally asked herself, seriously, if she should stop trail running. The question led to an uneasy acceptance. If she had spent the last twenty years running on city streets, she figures, more bad things would have happened, and she wouldn't have stood atop nearly so many mountains. She tells herself that while she could say that she had two frightening lion encounters in a year, she could also say she had *only* two in twenty years.

But Lucy is now certain that she will meet a lion again, that Cuyamaca's lions look at people with the same predator's gaze with which they survey deer. When she confronts the next lion, she's decided, she will live. And the cat will die.

16
The Best Cougar Story

Photo courtesy of Heather Cowley

Ron Receveur wonders why his dog, Buck, is still alive after their encounter with a cougar outside Port Alberni, B.C.

Ron Receveur's short, powerful build bespeaks a man who works hard, which is what Port Albernians do. He holds his muscular arms slightly bent, as though at any moment he might encounter a heavy load that needs carrying. A working man's tan turns his blue eyes to calm ocean water.

Port Alberni, British Columbia, population 20,000, lies near Vancouver Island's west coast. It calls itself "The Town with a Heart." Port Alberni was once a fishing and logging boomtown. Now times are harder, but people aren't complaining much. They like living here.

Ron's hometown is divided by four creeks running west out of the mountains, each densely wooded and deeply gullied, each with its own trail system and teenager hideaways. Each funnels wildlife right into the town's picturesque heart. Kitsuksis Creek carves the north edge of town. Rogers, Dry, and Shipp Creeks run through the middle. Partly because of those creeks, it seems that every Port Albernian has a strange animal encounter story. Unreported to authorities but passed about like spare change, they color the zeitgeist of the town.

In 1992, a cougar nabbed a little dog right downtown and carried it up a tree. Amazingly, the dog survived. Ron Receveur once saw two cougars walking down Shipp Creek Road about a half block from the street's first houses. Black bears are seen more often than cougars, probably because they are more active during the day, and because there are, according to official estimates, nearly ten times as many bears as cougars on Vancouver Island. During 1998's fall salmon feast, hundreds of partygoers wandered toward the festival grounds up one side of a finger-shaped inlet. On the far side, a black bear also wandered upstream, searching for fish entrails. Only the tourists stopped to stare.

Residents don't mind the bears. The island has never had a serious bear attack. But Vancouver Island is a hot zone for cougar attacks, and Port Albernians don't like cougars. They say the big cats are unpredictable in ways bears are not.

Local concern about cougars may explain why, when a childlike retarded man named Lloyd Dayton was found face-down in Kitsuksis Creek one hot July afternoon in 1995, blame fell on a cougar. Port Alberni already had one unexplained murder in its past, a local child whose abduction was almost certainly the work of a resident. Nobody wanted another.

Still, some officials were certain Lloyd Dayton's killer was no cougar. Cougar kills have a look, and Lloyd Dayton didn't fit it. He was found floating in a shallow pool, not buried in debris. His wounds were unobtrusive, a scatter of pencil-thick punctures on his neck, no obvious claw or bite marks. His brand-new red bike helmet, proudly shown off to friends earlier that day, was still strapped to his head, not a scratch on it.

If Lloyd Dayton had been killed by a cougar, he was the first person in recorded history attacked within a town of any size. Hunters with trained hounds searched for weeks. Residents were encouraged to call in every cougar sighting. The *Port Alberni Valley Times* repeatedly warned people about cougars and other wildlife in town.

Eighteen months passed. Then the newspaper exploded in outrage. It had just learned that the killing was being investigated as a homicide and probably had been for months. Suddenly Lloyd Dayton was no longer the island's fourth cougar death in less than two decades, but little Port Alberni's second unexplained murder.

The town had spent those months waiting for a killer cougar to strike, forbidding its children from playing in the creeks, peering through kitchen windows before taking out the trash on dark nights. An even stronger distrust of cougars had developed. The belated truth, that Port Alberni's most dangerous predator was human, wasn't likely to make it go away.

Since then, cougar-phobia hasn't faded. Stories like Ron Receveur's keep it alive.

Lloyd Dayton had been dead more than two years on the October morning Ron Receveur decided to try a favorite mushrooming spot on the lower slopes of Mount Arrowsmith, just outside of town. It was pine mushroom season, and this was a good year for pines. Ron had been finding an unusual number of big number ones, their caps still closed into spheres and worth top dollar. On this day, Ron knew, buyers were paying $12 a pound for number ones. With a little luck, he would make hundreds of dollars by sundown.

Maggie, Ron's long-time canine companion, had an appointment at the vet, so Ron decided to take her goofy son, Buck, for company. Buck looks nothing like his slim, alert border collie mom, except for his glossy black coat and white-splashed chest. His Labrador retriever father gave him a bigger frame—Buck weighs 75 pounds—and a Lab's gentle eyes. But he moves dodgy, like a cow dog.

"He's the fastest Lab I ever had," Ron likes to say. "But he's dumber than a bag of hammers."

That morning, Ron tossed his caulked boots into the van. Designed for loggers who work on steep terrain, they have steel "corks" spiked into heavy soles. He pulled on his surveyor's vest. Its pockets contained a water bottle, a small first-aid kit, a wood chisel, and a hunting knife.

Ron has been picking for twenty years, since long before mushroom hunting became a staple for the townspeople. Now, in late summer and fall, when first the chanterelles and then the pine mushrooms pop up, commercial mushroom buyers journey to Port Alberni to set up their scales, and locals head for the mountain slopes to make the easiest money they'll come by all year. Ron, old hand that he is, tries to get there first.

A short drive through quiet morning streets and Ron and Buck were out of the van, trudging straight up Mount Arrowsmith. The slope was so steep it felt like climbing stairs. The band of forest they struggled through had been logged years before and consisted of 30-foot-tall second-growth Douglas firs, laced together by shiny-leafed salal, scratchy wild rose, slim maple, willow, and alder. Branches slapped Ron's face and snapped against the two nested five-gallon buckets he hoped to fill with mushrooms. Ron could hear Buck zigzagging through the underbrush nearby, but seldom saw him among the twiggy, leafy tangle. The dog seemed to be staying closer than usual, perhaps 30 feet off. Ron wondered if the young dog felt insecure without Maggie to buddy with.

The break into what Ron calls "timber" was sudden and sweet. This part of the mountain had never been logged. Here the trees were wide-spaced old giants, with rich loam underfoot and a feeling of weighty peace, as among the stone pillars of a cathedral. This was where the pine mushrooms grew.

Ron began the mushroom hunter's methodical, zigzagging

search up the steep mountainside. He focused on the ground near his feet, training his eyes to the infrequent sight of brown-scaled white caps. Ron was vaguely aware that Buck was still running about in that goofy, oblivious way of his, nose locked to the ground, but staying close. Mostly though, Ron hunted.

Slowly his bucket filled as Ron found first one sparse patch, and then another. Bruised mushrooms aren't worth much, so he pried each stem gently from the ground with his wood chisel. With the first bucket full, Ron unstacked the second. Now, when he stopped to pick, he placed the full bucket against his leg so it wouldn't spill big, firm number ones down the steep slope.

Then Ron hit a bonanza, a picker's dream. He was in an area where the venerable trees were 40 feet apart. A few rotting logs littered the ground. Otherwise it was mossy and bare—except for the pine mushrooms, which seemed to be everywhere. Ron found a shallow depression where he could safely leave the full bucket and began happily topping the second.

The task was nearly complete when he noticed something odd. A log, 3 feet wide and 60 feet long, was propped over a shallow draw just uphill. This log had legs, four big, thick legs.

Fanatic that he is, Ron's first, disappointed thought was that another picker had stumbled upon this rare wealth of mushrooms, and he was seeing the person's dog. That thought was almost instantly shoved aside, though, by the size of those legs. They were too powerful looking. Those legs could belong to nothing but a cougar.

"Oh, shit," he thought. Ron was from Port Alberni, so he didn't feel awe, wish for a camera, or thank his stars for a sighting as rare as the mushroom patch in which he stood. Instead, his head filled with all the things he'd heard a person was supposed to do to keep from getting hurt: get big, get loud, don't run away.

A second passed. Then the cat's head appeared where its legs had been. Its eyes were locked on Buck. The dog stopped his sniffing explorations and turned to Ron as though asking a question. Then Buck followed Ron's eyes to the cat and began to whine. It felt to Ron like a signal: all hell was about to break loose. Figuring he'd make his move first, Ron began whacking his bucket with the chisel. An instant later, the cougar slipped below the log, fast and smooth as though skating on its belly. It aimed straight at Buck. Buck ran too, straight at Ron, whimpering as he came. If Buck stopped when he got to Ron, Ron was in trouble. But if Buck kept going, he was a dead dog. Ron found himself almost idly wondering which it would be.

The young dog passed three feet to Ron's right. The cougar glided by too, a body-length behind. Ron could have touched the tawny animal, but it seemed to see only Buck. The scene was made even more surreal by the fact that neither animal ran full-out. The goofy dog's tail was up like a flag, as though they played a game of tag, and the cougar's lope seemed designed to keep the distance steady, not to close it. Maybe it didn't know what to do with a dog that didn't understand it was about to die. Slow or fast though, this chase could end one way only.

"See ya, Buck," Ron thought sadly, and wondered how he would tell his wife.

Not because he feared for himself—the cougar wanted Buck, not him—but because his body was buzzing and thumping with adrenaline, Ron flung himself downhill, away from whatever was about to happen to Buck. One part of his mind listened for the horrible yelping to begin. Most of the rest focused on keeping his booted feet beneath him. Nevertheless, Ron managed to grab the other bucket by its metal bale as he half-slid, half-ran past, so that now he stumbled down the mountain with 15 pounds of mushrooms hanging from each arm.

For several minutes, Ron descended through forest silence. Then that silence was broken by the click and slide of rock on rock, right behind him. His mind supplied an image: the cougar frozen in midleap, aimed like an arrow at the back of Ron's head. He spun, heart in his throat. But it was Buck that ran at him, tongue hanging, tail wagging.

Fast behind came the cougar.

Ron lifted both buckets over his head, yelling wordlessly. The cat slowed and began circling. Ron set his buckets against his legs, grabbed two rocks and threw. He missed. The cougar's eyes never left the dog at his feet, but gradually its orbit widened.

The cat was 75 feet away when it entered a jumble of windfall. Instantly it became a shadow among shadows. Ron could see its long, graceful shape. But if he hadn't known it was there, he was pretty sure his gaze would have passed over it.

Buck remained pressed against his leg. Ron was glad, because he thought the dog was safe as long as he stayed close. Now that Buck had somehow made it back unharmed, the man was determined not to give the cougar a second chance. He would get Buck out of there.

Ron began feeling his way once more downhill, this time more cautiously. Something in the cat's stare made him not want to stumble. Nearly crouched, his hand brushed the ground, and touched something soft and smooth. The action was reflex: he picked the pine. He saw another, picked it. The third broke in his hand, rendering it unsellable.

"This is crazy," he thought. Perhaps that was when Ron realized it was no longer Buck that the cougar's eyes followed. Ron was standing around picking mushrooms while a cougar toyed with him.

So began the pair's second escape. They rushed, slipping and stumbling, down the slope. The dog stayed at his leg. The cat glided easily down the mountain beside and just a little behind them.

After a few minutes, Ron lost sight of it. He didn't believe the cougar was gone, though. He began spinning around every dozen steps, lifting the buckets so as to appear big and intimidating. Every time, he was half-convinced that this spin would catch the cougar in midleap. Every time, he saw nothing but forest shadows.

By now he had his hunting knife in one hand and the chisel in the other. His plan, if the lion attacked, was to drop the buckets and stab it with both tools. He also thought about slamming a bucket over the cat's head as it sprang. But he rejected that plan because he couldn't make himself dump all those fine, plump number ones.

He kept up a constant yelling as they fled, hoping the noise would intimidate the cat. Because he needed something to say, he addressed Buck: "Buck I can't believe you're here. I can't believe you made it. We gotta get out of here, Buck." Then he'd spin around, buckets raised. Just in case.

They finally reached the road and then a few minutes later, the van, without seeing the cougar again. Ron unlocked the back door. Buck jumped in and Ron, instead of walking around to the driver's side, crawled in behind. Sighing with relief, he slammed the door. His legs were rubbery.

"Man, I can't believe you got away," he told his now unconcerned dog.

Ron's breathing had just slowed when movement caught his eye. He peered out the van's back window. It was the cougar.

It sauntered down the dirt road toward the vehicle. Gone was the powerful intensity of posture and stare. The big animal now looked like an improbably large house cat out for a stroll. It meandered to a stop 5 feet from the van. It sat. Its gaze wandered here and there. Its front paws were tucked neatly together. It didn't seem aware that Ron and Buck were so close, literally an arm's reach away, but that closeness hypnotized Ron. He stared, unbelieving, through the small, dusty window.

But he couldn't stare forever, not even at a cougar that had chased him off the mountain and trailed him to his van. So after several minutes, Ron moved up to the driver's seat. For a while longer, he stared at the animal's image in his rearview mirror.

"I may's well go," Ron finally told himself, and turned the ignition key. The cat hastily backed away and disappeared off the road's brushy downhill side.

After stopping by his house to clean the mushrooms, Ron drove back out to sell them. He was in a hurry to warn his usual buyer, Paulette, so she could let other pickers know. Besides, he was dying to tell this story. Nobody had a cougar story this good.

But Paulette beat him to it. "I hear there was a cougar nosing around your van today," she said.

"How d'you know that?" he asked, confused. He had mentioned the cougar to his sister when she stopped by, but his sister didn't know Paulette.

"A couple other pickers were in; they saw a cougar by your van early this morning."

"Early this morning?"

"Yeah, first thing."

For the first time, Ron felt real fear. Buck and Ron hadn't stumbled upon a cougar in the old growth forest of Mount Arrowsmith, accidentally putting a rude end to an otherwise fine day of picking. They had been followed every step of the way.

As the pair had forced their way through second growth so dense twenty cougars could have hidden in it, as Ron zigzagged among the old growth, eyes primed to see only mushrooms — for three hours or more, they had been followed. Ron remembered how Buck had stayed close all morning, as though he knew.

It was really true: nobody in Port Alberni had a cougar story this good.

17
Stalked

Cougar tracks shadow the trail of a lone cross-country skier in Montana's Swan Valley.

Bowhunter Steve Carmichael was scouting for elk in eastern Oregon in the fall of 1999 when he noticed an acrid odor. It reminded him of old kitty litter. Then he saw the cougar lying in a slight depression 10 feet away. It snarled and disappeared into the brush.

Shaken, Steve decided to leave. He crossed a small creek, then walked more than half a mile before reaching a barbed wire fence. There he sat to rest and think about what he'd seen—and noticed a large brown animal standing in the trail he'd just left. It stared at him. Unbelievable: the second cougar sighting of his life, barely ten minutes after the first. Could it be the same one? If so, didn't that mean it had followed him?

Fighting an urge to flee, he instead rose, lifted his bow above his head and growled. The cougar simply stared back. That was when Steve noticed, behind the big cat, a spotted kitten. Bears defend their young. Maybe cougars did, too. Steve got more nervous. Then, as if in an Indiana Jones movie, another full-sized cougar appeared behind the first two. This was way, way too much.

Steve took two careful steps backward. The nearest, largest cat took two steps forward.

Steve glanced down to nock an arrow. In that brief moment, the cougar shortened the distance between them. Steve stepped-back again, and as he did, he couldn't help but glance behind him to check for rocks or logs. When he looked up, the cat had glided closer yet.

If someone were about to be hurt, Steve decided, he'd rather it be the cougar. He let fly. The cougar crouched; the arrow whizzed past. As if it had neither seen the arrow's motion nor heard its landing clatter, the animal simply continued to stare. The man shot again. This arrow grazed the cat's left shoulder. It ran into the forest, followed by its companions.

Two days and five miles farther into their annual family hunt, Steve's son Greg starred in the sequel. Scouting alone, Greg faced first one, and then a second full-sized cougar. He yelled, cursed, and raised his bow over his head. Steve heard his son's shouts through the fading light, "Get out of here. Go away. Leave me alone!" Greg fired an arrow, but missed. One after the other, the cougars left. Feeling outnumbered, Steve and Greg decided to end their hunting trip early.

Some call them stalkings. Others dislike the word because it implies an unproven assumption that the animal hunts the human it follows. The facts are these: most serious cougar attacks begin from ambush, not from a staring confrontation; and no human who has been stalked but not attacked can know if attack was imminent. However, those who've had this experience say that being followed by a predator has a way of making a person feel like prey.

Consider these four recent stories, which define the range of disturbing cougar encounters. What sets them apart from incidental sightings is that the cat seems to be in charge. What makes them different from attacks is that the cougar never makes physical contact, although it may do everything but. While they seldom involve more than one cat—in that, the Carmichaels' twin encounters are bizarre—stalking encounters are not uncommon. Stories like these can be found with a quick search through the archives of any western newspaper. These happen to come from Spokane, Washington's daily, the *Spokesman-Review*, whose circulation area includes rich deer and cougar habitat.

Shaun Johnson, dropping newspapers for delivery outside Spokane at 3:30 A.M., glanced up to see a cougar emerge from the woods. Although it could have circled through forest, invisible, the animal instead walked across open ground, right past Shaun, and continued toward the lakefront homes the papers were destined for. It showed no interest in the man, but no fear, either. Shaun nervously hopped into his van, shut the door, and watched the animal glide across his rearview mirror.

A Forest Service worker hiking alone one morning had a more intimidating experience. He was followed by a cougar for thirty minutes at a distance of perhaps 30 yards. The animal sometimes circled the man and sometimes trailed him, but never approached. It disappeared before other Forest Service workers arrived.

Russell Maas and his fourteen-year-old nephew were scouting for game near Moyie Springs, Idaho, when a cougar burst from the brush, sprinting straight at them. It stopped 10 yards away, crouched, and growled. The two yelled and waved their arms, but the cougar didn't budge. Finally Russell, remembering an old cougar hunter tale, barked like a dog. The cougar fled and was not seen again.

Darrell Brazington and his adult stepson were approached by a cougar as they surveyed timber near Priest River, Idaho. The men tried barking, waving their arms, and yelling, but the big cat kept coming. Finally, Darrell told his stepson to take off his shirt. They wrapped it around a stick and set it afire. The cougar wheeled away from the makeshift torch, but shadowed the men at a distance of 50 feet as they hiked to safety.

These encounters made newspaper headlines because the people involved reported them. But most people who capture cougars' attention do not report their encounters: they don't know they had them. Cougar hunter Bob Sheppard followed a cat's track one night into a new rural subdivision near Missoula, Montana. Standing in the cougar's shallow, round prints, he stared into a lit basement window. He was sure that the animal, too, had paused to stare inside. Then he followed the tracks across the backyard and out of the subdivision. He figured that the homeowners, who had driven away perhaps 45 minutes earlier, had probably been watched as they climbed into their vehicle.

Cougar hunters often find, as they retrace their steps homeward, that the day's freshest cougar sign lies atop their own bootprints. Although this happens often enough that cougar hunters joke about it, it's a rare hunter who actually sees the trailing animal.

"How can I be out in the hills as much as I am and never see [cougars]? There's a fascination in the fact that I can't see them, but they're watching me," muses longtime Montana houndsman Ed Roche.

In the sparsely populated central Montana country Ed hunts, cougars are easy to find. He could tree a cat almost every good tracking day, if he wanted. But he has never seen a cougar his dogs didn't chase up for him. He and his hunting friends have many, many photographs, even videotape, of wild cougars. But the subjects are all in trees with hounds barking up at them.

"If a cougar follows you really close, you might see it. But if he stays 25 yards away, you'll probably never know," says Idaho houndsman Steve Ryan.

Cougars and cougar stories abound in the tiny central Idaho town of Lowell where Steve and his wife Anne live. The Ryans run a small café called the Wilderness Inn. On one wall hangs an 8-foot-long cougar hide, its head and densely furred tail still attached. The long canines are curved. Even the molars are as sharp-edged as a mountain skyline. The fur is slightly coarser than a housecat's, short and neat. In plain view across the river is the glass phone booth in which, says Anne, a camper once took refuge as a cougar prowled past and into a busy resort's grassy campground.

Anne likes to tell a local story about two hunters scouting for game on parallel ridgelines. One man fired his weapon in the direction of the other, a friendship-straining offense to say the least. Later, the shooter reduced his irate companion to stunned silence by explaining that he'd fired at a cougar ghosting close behind the man.

Hunting guide, tracker, and houndsman Tom Parker lives in Montana's Swan Valley. He believes cougars have a natural aversion to humans that makes us unattractive as prey, but says, "It's not at all uncommon for cats to . . . investigate humans."

Tom chooses his words carefully. "Stalk," or even "follow," sounds too alarmist. Tom wants to give cougars the benefit of the doubt. Particularly, he points out, since cougars have many, many opportunities to attack people and don't.

"If I were a lion and I looked at these helpless, slow-moving, unobservant beings, I don't think I'd resist the temptation," says Tom. Yet cougars do exactly that, he notes, all the time.

Tom has a stalking story, too. One spring day, he was scouting for bear on a steep, west-facing slope. Logged off long ago, the slope was shrubby and dotted with 10-foot-tall ponderosa pines, which made visibility poor. Movement drew his eye to a half-dozen mule deer bunched together. They were staring intently at a point below Tom and to his right. Tom knows to pay attention to animal eyes; they show him things. Sure enough, concealed beneath a pine tree 70 yards from Tom and watched nervously by the deer was a mountain lion. At almost the same moment that Tom saw the lion, it caught sight of him through the brush and began gliding toward him.

Tom thought he knew what was happening. With their several pairs of eyes all focused on the cat, the deer were difficult prey. Tom, on the other hand, was alone and too obscured by foliage to be identified. The hunter stepped left, trying to make himself visible through a break in the brush. The cougar responded by turning into a shallow draw.

A less savvy woodsman might have thought the lion gone, but Tom realized that the draw could bring the animal, unseen, nearly to his feet. It wasn't leaving; it was still hunting. Tom turned to face the spot where, if he had guessed right, the cougar would appear. Minutes later, a round head emerged from the brush. The eyes were riveted to Tom.

"I'm confident that cat didn't know I was human," says Tom. "It had only seen little movements through the brush. I was apprehensive, but thought that once it realized what I was, I could deter it."

The hunter stepped up onto a log. "Hey, you. Get out of here," he yelled. The cat instantly deflated, spun toward its tail, and disappeared.

It seems Tom was right. This cougar did not want to hunt a human, but is that true of other stalking cats? If so, why do they follow humans at all? What's in it for them?

In the early spring of 1999, Tom and his wife, Mel, took the authors of this book looking for cats. A day-old dusting over a firm snow base made for good tracking, and the party soon crossed fresh sign. But the animal's wide, round footprints were not the only marks on the isolated logging road. The cat's tracks paralleled—and sometimes lay atop—the twin rails left by a lone cross-country skier.

With practiced grace, Tom produced a tape measure. A few moments later he announced that the tracks had probably been left by an adult female. Adult males are a third larger than females, with proportionately larger paws and a longer stride.

To find out how the cougar came to place her feet in the skier's trail, the group back-trailed her. Ten minutes' snowshoeing led into dense forest and finally to a cougar daybed, an irregular oval depression in the snow beneath a fir. It was situated on a hillside so heavily used by deer that the cold mountain air was sharp with their scent.

From this, the trail's beginning, Tom read the story in the snow. The cat had exploded from her bed with huge bounds of 12 feet or more. Then she slowed to a ground-eating trot aimed straight at the logging road, which was invisible but only a quarter mile away. Tom speculated aloud that the cougar had heard the skier's shush, shushing, and hurried to investigate.

The two trails first met near where we had initially crossed them. The cat's track followed the skier's from that point for 200 yards. Then the cougar's veered left, back into heavy forest. The skier's trail continued out of sight around a bend in the road.

She got bored, we said. Tom simply turned to follow the round paw prints into the trees. Why did he look so smug? It all became clear when we realized that her track made a beeline through the brush, effectively shortcutting the switchback. After the curve, the cat's tracks rejoined the skier's.

Her next shortcut bypassed a massive squiggling meander in the old logging road. It saved her perhaps a mile. On a high bank before she rejoined the road, Tom found the cougar's only stopping place of the journey. She had stood, perhaps for quite a while, shifting her feet now and then but not sitting or crouching. Did she wait for the skier, now behind her because of the shortcut, to glide past? If so, she gave up and stepped onto the road too early, because for a short distance the cat's tracks were *beneath* the skier's.

Interpreting Cougar Body Language

Cougar sightings can be broken into categories.
In each type of encounter, cougar body language
seems to send a clear message.

Incidental Sighting

The most common cougar sighting. The cougar is glimpsed dodging out of sight. It doesn't hold eye contact.

RISK: Extremely low. It is not necessary to report this sighting, except in or near a populated area.

Intentional Encounter

The cougar strolls by or lies near people. It does not stare at them, but is aware of their presence and shows no desire to leave.

RISK: Low. Rashes of such sightings have preceded attacks, but immediate danger is probably low. This bold cougar should be reported, especially in or near an area of high human traffic.

Stalking

The cougar remains nearby, holding eye contact in a way usually described as staring or glaring. It may face people, follow, or circle them. It maintains a steady distance, neither approaching nor slipping away.

RISK: Moderate to high. It is unclear how many attacks have been preceded by stalking, but many stalking incidents escalate into confrontation. This cougar should be reported immediately. Other people in the area should be alerted.

Confrontation

Some confrontations begin when the cougar is spotted running at a person, ears forward and eyes locked on the individual. More often, the cougar is first seen standing on a trail or at the edge of a campsite or following a person. The cougar continues to stare, but gradually or suddenly changes posture. Its ears tuck. Its mouth may be slightly open, revealing its teeth. It may snarl, almost always silently. Its tail tip may twitch. It may sink into a crouch. Crouching may be followed by bluff charges.

RISK: High. Confrontations have escalated into attacks. This cougar should be reported immediately. Other people in the area should be alerted.

Source: Authors' survey of attack reports 1990–1999, in conjunction with authors' compilation of recent encounters and sightings.

A dozen yards later, the animal had leaped aside into dense brush, and then returned to the road. Now the cat's tracks were again atop those of the skier, as though she had hidden to let the skier pass so she could again follow.

A half-mile later, the cougar left the road again, this time for good. She headed into a thicket, where layers of tracks said she often spent time. Deer trails laced the area as well.

Tom points out that this cat used a good part of her day to follow the skier, ultimately without bothering the lone human. More interesting yet, she knew the skier would stay on the road, and that shortcutting the road would intersect the track again. How? She had to have watched people, and not just casually. She had watched often enough to be able to predict human actions.

Some stalkings, especially in remote areas, seem very different from this one, as if the cats are puzzling out a creature they have never before encountered.

In August of 1996, a young river guide named Dave O'Keefe hitchhiked up central Idaho's Lochsa River to a trailhead he had used before on his regular solitary backpacks. Across the Lochsa sprawled the Selway-Bitterroot Wilderness, one of the few places in the country still wild enough to support grizzlies. Dave headed away from designated wilderness and toward country just as wild: Clearwater country, one of the most arduous legs of the original Lewis and Clark Trail.

Five miles in, he reached the flat area where he had planned to camp. An old miner's cabin shared the brushy clearing. Dave figured that was because the builder had had no choice: in this rugged country, there were no other flat spots for miles.

Always careful about attracting wildlife, Dave hung his food from the log bridge that crossed Fish Creek. Then he laid out his bedding. Not much for tents, Dave liked trees and sky for bedroom walls and ceiling.

At 3:00 A.M. the young man woke with a vague sense of urgency. He took stock. He lay on his back, legs straight, arms tucked into his mummy bag against the damp mountain chill. No sound disturbed the stillness. He let his eyes open, and felt his heart accelerate immediately: above and behind his head, something blocked stars. A dog, he thought. A wolf? Whatever it was, it was too damn close.

He was afraid to free his hands—the zipper would buzz—so he rolled rapidly to his knees, facing what stood motionless, facing him. That was when he realized it was a full-grown, honest-to-God cougar.

The cat backed away two steps and Dave, heart thudding, began talking quietly, "Take it easy, buddy. Take it easy."

Enough moonlight pooled in the clearing that Dave could begin to make out the animal's tensed muscles and narrowed eyes. It didn't look any happier than he was. If it attacked, Dave told himself, he'd duke it in the nose. "I grew up surfing in shark-infested waters and that's what I'd always heard, give 'em one good punch in the nose and they'll go away."

The fact that his hands were still trapped in the sleeping bag didn't register with the 5-foot-5-inch, 130-pound man until much later. The fact that the cat looked huge did. Twenty seconds passed. Then its muscles visibly relaxed. It turned and paced slowly toward the black wall of forest.

Dave knew the encounter was over. The cat's body language was telling him so. Fear evaporated, and he began trying to record what suddenly seemed a painfully lovely thing, the cat lit by moonlight, its body gracefully still, carried by legs rolling forward and feet placed with light, silent precision. He wished it would look back so he could memorize its face as well. It didn't.

Hear enough of these stories, and you find yourself begging for answers. Stalkings are a recurring and important part of the cougar-human dynamic. Yet any animal who, over time, expends more energy than it consumes will die. And plenty of cougars do starve, bankrupted by this harsh accounting system. What does the cougar mean to accomplish, then, by stalking us? Why waste the energy? Are stalkings attacks that almost happened? Are attacks stalking incidents during which the human did something wrong?

*Montana research houndsman Tom Parker measures a cougar's stride
to estimate the animal's gender and age.*

The search for reasonable answers is stymied by the comforting
but false belief that cougars have an innate or learned fear of
humans. Why would a pinnacle predator carry an inborn fear of a
soft, hairless creature with poor hearing and no useful sense of
smell? A cougar who has had a chance to learn a fear of humans is
probably dying at the base of a tree.

Longtime cougar hunters Steve Ryan and Doug Caltrider
believe that the cats have a natural fear of hounds but not of the
hunters themselves. This makes sense, since the dog's distant
cousin, the wolf, has for thousands of years used its superior
numbers to steal cougar kills and even kill cougars.

Doug once stayed to watch a treed tom after the dogs were
led away.

"It was just like you flipped a switch back on," he says. "He'd
been cowering on a branch and then he stood up, pricked his ears,

and looked down as if to say, 'Buddy, I ain't scared of you. I'm not up here 'cause of you.'"

Here's one possible explanation for cougar stalkings. Predators like African lions and wolves sometimes show themselves to prey before attacking. Some think the predator watches for a fear reaction. An animal that shows no fear may be telegraphing the fact that it is healthy and alert, a difficult adversary. The fearful animal may betray, by its fear, the fact that it is less able to flee or fight effectively. Naturalist Barry Lopez has even wondered in *Of Wolves and Men* if predator and prey don't collaborate in the moments before an attack. An ill or old caribou might be grateful for a fast finish instead of slow starvation, says Lopez, and the wolf grateful for being pointed to an easy, safe kill.

If cougars are like these predators, stalking and charging could be the cougar's attempt to ask the all-important question, "Are you my meat?" Perhaps, unable to see ourselves from within the food chain, we send back unreadable answers. The animal follows, encouraged neither to attack nor to give up.

Or it could be that cougars are confused by similarities and differences between humans and deer. Cougars seem to be hardwired to prefer deer. Everywhere the two species live, the one eats the other. And humans, like deer, can be found along trails or in clearings. Both humans and deer are often found near water. Both travel in groups. Individuals have approximately the same mass.

But they are not the same shape, which, some believe, is why cougar attacks are so rare. Perhaps cautious cougars hesitate to attack something large that lacks the four legs and long, ungulate neck of a deer, features which trigger a hard-wired attraction. So the cougar studies humans out of interest but keeps a safe distance out of caution.

Perhaps stalking has nothing to do with hunting. Wolves and dogs use stiff-legged displays to assert and hold social position in a pack. Bears posture to keep the best fishing spot in a river or to warn other bears away from cubs. Bear attacks upon humans are often preceded by warnings like loud jaw popping or swaying on the hind legs. It seems likely that humans attacked after such warnings weren't able to respond in ways that satisfied the bear. If, for instance, the correct response from another bear would have been a noisy twenty-five-mile-per-hour retreat, the human's fumbling backward walk might appear insultingly casual.

If cougars communicate among themselves about who has to leave an area and who gets to stay, perhaps stalking and charging are part of the vocabulary. Stalking could be a cougar's response when a human doesn't acknowledge an attempt at communication—a scent marker perhaps—which the human couldn't "read." A cougar crouched on a road bank, staring intently at a person, may be screaming in cougarese, "Can't you hear me? Get the hell off my porch, you social incompetent. You're scaring away my deer."

Author Richard Conniff offers a friendlier explanation for stalkings, courtesy of biologist Sarah Durant of the Serengeti Cheetah Research Project. Watching two cheetahs, bellies still rounded with a recent meal, who stopped to observe antelope and wildebeest but did not give chase, Sarah said, "I often think they watch prey the way we watch television, because it's comforting and mindless."

We can support Sarah's theory with observations made much closer to home. Domestic cats, close relatives of the cougar, show endless interest in things that move. Perhaps a moving human interests a cougar in the same way a drifting leaf or a goldfish in a bowl interests a housecat.

A question needs asking here, though. In housecats or cougars, is this curiosity idle entertainment or does it reflect a more purposeful interest? Paul Leyhausen and others have experimented with housecats and captive wild species and found that a cat will chase, catch, and kill mice long after it is full. After a while, it may stop killing, but will continue chasing and catching. Then it may stop catching, but will continue to chase.

Why? Think about what successful hunters do with their time. Most predators chase more animals than they catch, and catch more than they manage to kill. If they are females with young, they kill more than they eat. The same is true if other predators steal their kills. If only the eating gave pleasure, most of the predator's life would be unsatisfying. So it may be that successful predators are rewarded at every step in the hunt, from stalk to kill to belly full of meat, with a sensation we might recognize as joy.

Are people who are stalked in danger? Almost certainly yes. No matter why the cougar follows, a predator can't afford to go long without killing. At some point as it silently trails a hiker down a brushy path, it must consider its options. And one of the most fascinating facts about cougars is that after minutes or hours of shadowing a human whose senses are too weak to tell him he's not alone, this terrifyingly effective predator almost always silently strolls away.

18
Hard Truths

Photo by Dave Fjelline

By turns ferocious and easily intimidated, cougars don't make simple neighbors.

In 1998, Wes Collins lived in forested foothills outside Issaquah, a bedroom community to Seattle. Washington State has had its share of well-publicized cougar attacks, almost all of them on children. But Wes didn't worry much about his four kids: he had a dog. Then in May of 1998, a 145-pound cougar attacked and killed his part-Labrador retriever within a few yards of the house. It dragged the dog's body 50 yards into cover. The next morning when state Fish and Wildlife agents arrived, the cougar was still there. Agents tried to tree it with their hounds, but it attacked those dogs as well, according to the *Seattle Times*.

It's an understandable error to think a family dog ensures against cougar attack. Cougars, after all, are hunted with hounds, from which they nearly always flee. Less well-known is the fact that they regularly kill and eat dogs of all sizes. What's more, researchers have documented cases where dogs led the cougars that pursued them straight back to their owners, just as Ron Receveur's dog, Buck, did. People in cougar country make other understandable safety errors as well. Some of these errors add to their risk, others to the outrage they feel when something they have decided won't happen does.

For instance, some think that if their pets don't protect them, they can at least protect their pets. A fence, perhaps, or a leash, or just keeping an eye on them will keep domestic animals from harm. But it's not that easy. California biologist and author Steven Torres believes pet attacks are one of the fastest growing cougar problems, possibly even a precursor to attacks on humans. Pets are taken from yards, decks, and porches. Some, on morning strolls with their owners, are yanked right out of their collars. One cougar walked into a mountain resort's store through the open back door to snatch a puppy playing at a woman's feet.

Twenty-year-old Joshua Rhoden was running three dogs, including a half-grown rottweiler-chow, behind his truck near Olympic National Park in Washington State, when he saw a huge, tawny animal bounding behind the dogs. The cougar grabbed the stocky pup and sprang into a roadside ditch. Joshua stopped and ran back to throw rocks and scream at the cougar, but it did not release the dog. Joshua finally got scared and gave up, said the *Peninsula Daily News*.

Horses seem way too big to be in danger from an animal that seldom weighs more than 150 pounds. And while it's true that cougars seldom attack horses, they do attack people on horse-back. Little Steven Parolin was taken off his horse by a cougar before he was mauled. Californian Lona Kottle was riding in Cuyamaca Rancho State Park when her horse began tipping its ears nervously toward the dense brush. She knew she had company, but not that her visitor was a cougar until it intercepted her at a high cutbank. The cougar backed off only after she charged her horse at it. In these cases and others, the cat showed no interest in the horse. It focused on the human.

These days, cougar country is awash with advice about how to handle encounters. It is broadcast on local television and printed in the newspaper, especially after an attack or rash of sightings. Warning signs mark trailheads, and park visitor centers stock cougar safety pamphlets. But sound bites, signs, and leaflets can be misleading because they are, of necessity, short and simple. Safety among large predators is not simple. The warnings are also easy to think too little about. Living honestly with the slim but inescapable risk of attack is no fun. It means checking your assumptions. It means giving up carefree days in the woods. It means looking over your shoulder.

Noise and human bustle make people feel more secure, partly because intuition says it should, and partly because cougar safety brochures advise hikers and runners to travel with others. But while groups are a good idea, they don't prevent all attacks, especially not on kids. Sixteen of nineteen 1990s child victims were in groups when attacked. Some were in large, noisy clusters, hiking at the end of a line of children and camp counselors, like Dante Swallow, or running through a church camp with other children, like the little girl attacked by a half-grown kitten in Hope, British Columbia.

That's why another typical cougar country warning—to keep children close—can be misleading. There is a good reason to keep kids close and to travel in groups around cougars, but it's not because companions *prevent* attack. The reason is that companions can *end* attacks. In the 1990s, no child attacked while in the company of an adult has died.

Of the two kids that did die, one, Mark Miedema, was hiking minutes ahead of his parents when attacked. They arrived in time to see their son dragged, unresisting, from the trail. They chased the cougar away, but the boy was already dying. The other, a boy named Jeremy Williams, was sitting with three other kids at the edge of a schoolyard in Kyuquot, British Columbia. In the minute or two before the children's screams summoned adult help, fatal damage was done. The school custodian shot the cat off the boy. The eight-year-old breathed his last, jerky gasps cradled in his rescuer's arms.

One amazing fact that cougar safety brochures leave out altogether, perhaps to prevent lawsuits, is that rescuers are almost never badly hurt. They usually aren't even scratched. When bears attack, would-be rescuers become victims too, as though, like a barroom brawler, the provoked bear simply needs to fight and any target will do. It's an easy mistake to think cougars are the same, and several would-be rescuers have hung back, fearful of the claws and teeth that rip at their friend or family member.

But rescuers who face cougars sometimes find all they have to do to end the attack is shout. John Musselman was barefoot and empty-handed when he charged his son's attacker. The cat evaporated before him like a ghost. More often, rescuers must use force, but their weapons don't have to be fancy. Nine-year-old Darron Arroyo's dad smashed a rock onto the head of the cougar that was dragging his son away. Visibly stunned, the cougar dropped the boy and fled. In Nevada, Mary Saethre was rescued by one companion while another stood by, perhaps frozen by the understandable belief that a real weapon was needed, though he could find only a rock. Meanwhile, Paul Greger drove Mary's 70-pound attacker off by hitting it repeatedly with his camera. None of these rescuers reported receiving even a scratch. A daycare worker, weaponless, literally ripped a cougar from a child in her care. Although she was injured as the animal escaped her, the wounds were minor compared to those she prevented.

If it sounds odd that such a formidable predator could be

deterred with a camera, or that hand-to-hand combat with a cougar can have a happy ending, consider this: even a determined deer, under most circumstances the choicest of cougar meals, can stand off its nemesis, as raft guide Shane Duncan witnessed one summer day in 1997.

Shane was part of a commercial rafting and camping trip down the Snake River as it carves a rugged canyon border between Idaho and Oregon. The rafts had stopped at a spot called Deep Creek when guests noticed a doe and two fawns scrambling up a ravine on the river's far side. As the group watched the little family, one of the fawns suddenly tumbled downhill in a cloud of dust.

It took Shane a moment to realize that another animal had caused the tumble. In that moment, the doe attacked. She reared onto her hind legs, flailing with heart-shaped hooves, and forced whatever it was away from her fawn and into a low, brambly hackberry tree. She pawed the tree for several moments. Then she backed away to stand guard before the crumpled fawn.

The rafters were horrified and enthralled. Who would have thought a deer could fight off, well, whatever it was? Something small, Shane figured. Small enough to be afraid of a deer. Bobcat, maybe?

For fifteen minutes, the doe faced the tree. The little bobcat didn't budge. If the doe was hoping the fragile tangle of legs at her back would rise and rejoin its sibling, she waited in vain. It never stirred. Finally she turned, gathered her remaining fawn, and exited the ravine. The animal in the tree immediately bounded down, and Shane saw it clearly for the first time. It was big and long, with a brown stripe down its back and a long, thick brown tail. Not a bobcat at all, but something much more formidable. The cougar easily lifted the limp fawn by its neck and carried it behind a rock.

One of the most frightening aspects of a cougar attack also tends not to be mentioned in safety brochures, but it's what sticks in witnesses' and victims' minds: the animal's intense focus. Cougars don't watch the people they stalk, they stare. Cats chased from injured children return again and again. They try to sneak between rescuers' legs, as did the cougar that attacked Dante Swallow. They stop just out of kicking range and stare, as did the cat that attacked Justin Mellon in Caspers Wilderness Park. When Lila Lifely made the mistake of leaving the child she had rescued to retrieve first-aid gear, the cougar immediately returned. Much later, after help arrived, the cougar returned yet again. It's probably this unswerving focus that keeps most rescuers safe: the cougar simply couldn't care less about them. They are obstacles, nothing more.

Differences between predator species create confusion for those trying to coexist with cougars. For instance, playing dead is recommended in grizzly attacks. It's thought that the technique works because the bear is attacking to neutralize a threat. An unresponsive, prone person is not as threatening as one standing up. Some think playing dead should work with cougars, too. They're wrong. Those who've played dead for a cougar were simply dragged away.

Despite the fact that playing dead doesn't work and that, given the chance, cougars eat the people they kill, many still believe cougar attacks are defensive, not predatory. It makes cougars seem more likable. It makes people feel safer. Who wants to believe we are meat? One of the easiest ways to refute that misconception is to compare another piece of bear safety advice with cougar safety advice. Bears really do generally attack after being startled or in defense of young. So people who encounter tense bears are told never to make eye contact. Eye contact is an act of aggression, which increases the bear's perturbation. But cougars who confront people have already acted with predatory aggression. So cougar safety brochures tell people to maintain eye contact, and again and again, victims tell of attacks which began the instant eye contact was broken.

Andy Peterson, attacked in 1998 in Colorado's Roxborough State Park, locked eyes with a cougar at some distance for several minutes before momentarily breaking eye contact. In what seemed an instant, the once comfortably distant cougar was, literally, in his face.

Suzanne Groves was collecting stream samples when she noticed she was being eyed by a cougar. She began wading the shallow Mancos River toward her vehicle. The cat matched her, step for step. They danced warily back and forth across the river three or four times, staring at each other. The woman splashed water and yelled. The cat merely continued to pace her, continued to stare. Finally, the woman stumbled on slick rocks, and as she fell, lost sight of the cat. The next instant, Suzanne felt the animal bite into the back of her head, forcing her face underwater.

Luckily for Suzanne, the cougar was old, nearly toothless, and underweight at 63 pounds. The woman managed to wrestle herself on top of the cat. She ran, was tackled, wrestled herself on top again and finally stabbed the animal in the eye with a pair of forceps. When the cougar broke free, Suzanne backed carefully away and escaped to her vehicle.

Here's another misconception. Cougar brochures often point out that mountain lions hunt at night. California's Department of Fish and Game states in their *Living with California Mountain Lions* brochure that parents should "Make sure children are inside between dusk and dawn." Tips like this make it easy to assume that during the day, cougar country residents are safe. But probably because of sheer numbers—many, many times more humans are about in daylight than at night—most attacks occur during the day. In fact, it may be that the single biggest reason cougar attacks are rare is that we are creatures of the day and they are of the night. It may be that cougars seem shy not because they almost never hunt humans, but because they almost never hunt in daylight. If we shared the same hours, the cougar-human relationship might look very different.

Perhaps the most dangerous misconception people in cougar country have is the belief that, as an Idaho river guide once said, "If a mountain lion ever jumps me, I'll kick its ass." All it takes to correct that mistake are a few conversations with attack survivors. It's true that adults often fight off their attackers, but it's pure luck that allows them the opportunity. In most attacks, the victim's first

What people do when cougars strike

1990s attacks reveal how seldom victims were able to defend against attacking cougars, as well as the odds against averting an attack before it starts.

No action. Victim didn't see cat before
it struck, or saw the animal briefly
but had no time to act. 21

Watched the cat approach without
any defensive response 4

Panicked and ran 4

Backed away 2

Waved arms, yelled, threw things 2

Received injury in attempt to rescue
another victim 4

Unknown 16

Source: Authors' survey of attack reports 1990-1999.

inkling of trouble is a powerful blow from behind. Others glimpse the animal's charge, but too late to react. If that first hit stuns them, as almost certainly happened to Barbara Schoener and Iris Kenna, the victims never have a chance. In the 1990s, nearly one fourth of adults who were alone when attacked died.

The other three-fourths no longer have the luxury of cougar country's most common response to the risk of attack: disbelief. Deciding they won't ever be attacked makes people feel better, and for most it winds up true. But people who have faced cougars are forced into honesty, and honest, safe coexistence with large predators is no comfortable thing.

Epilogue

Results of one day's hunt, circa 1951.

It bears saying one last time: we didn't write this book because cougar attacks are common. They're not. Frankly, we began because there's no such thing as a boring cougar story. By the end, our reasons had become more serious.

Rare or not, cougar attacks are horrific. Lives are shattered in the blink of an eye. People deserve a chance to consider this before they hike, camp, or move their households into cougar country.

We have also become impatient with two camps in modern

environmentalism. The first paints large predators harmless, as though only harmless animals can be sold to the public. The second helps a once-persecuted predator recover in numbers, or sometimes even relocates them into a region, and then behaves as though nothing has changed about the way that region's residents will have to live their lives.

We believe realistic discussion of the cougar, sharp claws and all, is necessary if the species is to survive in a human-dominated world. The problem with realistic discussion has always been that it doesn't generate palatable answers. It yields unsettling ideas like these:

People who move into the rural or suburban West often buy a few chickens or a horse. They don't know that large predators still wander the hills. Or they know it, but don't see what it has to do with them. Then, when morning dawns on livestock carcasses, some demand action. The unpopular truth is that there are areas where it's plain irresponsible to own a few goats or llamas, just as many cities have areas that careful citizens avoid at night.

The even more unpopular truth is that there are areas where cougars should be allowed to be cougars, unhunted and undisturbed. Hornocker Institute researchers have proposed setting aside huge cougar refuges, what they call "biological savings accounts," to do just this. We believe humans using those areas should bend to cougar rules and accept cougar risks. Too often, people expect themselves, their pets, and their livestock to be safe in places that can't be made safe without an incredible cost to other species.

Conversely, there are areas where people *should* be safe from predator attack. Near most cities and many towns, cougars should be subject to human rules. Right now, cougars in and near cities are often ignored or relocated in a mistaken attempt to preserve the species or out of a belief that they will do no harm. Cougars are not harmless. They are hunters. Wherever they go, they shed blood. It can be a false kindness to let a young, near-town cougar live. If the cat, hungry and unable to find his preferred prey, kills a pet dog or a person, everybody loses.

Brochures, newspaper columns, and books are dedicated to helping people create backyard habitat for wild creatures. It's a pretty idea, but not necessarily a good one, especially in cougar country. When suburbanites put out a salt block for deer or cultivate garden plants that deer browse upon, they are inviting cougars to hunt in the shadows of their homes. Leaving garbage cans out invites raids from the cougar's smaller prey, raccoons, skunks, and opossums. On Vancouver Island, conservation officers have begun telling residents that when they report a scavenging bear or a wandering cougar, officers that respond will not relocate the animal. They'll kill it. Officers report a marked increase in people willing to solve their own problem, putting the dog and his food bowl inside, for instance.

A final point: California voters have, by outlawing cougar hunting, told their officials they want cougars to live. And yet in the Santa Ana Mountains of Southern California, cougars are dying off. Why? Because nobody oversees urban sprawl, road building, and their effects; because Californians care, but not enough to change how they develop those foothills.

Should the Santa Ana cougars live? Probably not. It's too late there. We didn't leave enough room. Should the species survive elsewhere? Some would say that question is moot: North Americans tried to kill cougars off for centuries and failed. But back then, cougars had vast strongholds to retreat to. In the United States today, no part of their world is more than 20 miles from a road.

It's not politically correct to wish a species extinct, but are extinctions so biologically tragic? They occurred long before humans became so good at engineering them. Biologists try hard to come up with objective, logical reasons why problematic species like cougars should survive. We've never heard one yet that can stand up to land developers' money or alleviate the anguish of a mutilated child. The fact is, if cougars became extinct tomorrow, in spite of any effect their absence would have on the web to which they belong, few humans would notice.

But we would know, right? There may be no unassailable argument for preserving a species that sees us as prey, whether grizzly bear, wolf, or cougar. But there are reasons.

We've proven again and again that we're not smart enough to monkey with a system as ancient and complex as the food chain. From cane toads to bull trout, our tinkering has produced repercussions terrifying to eighty-year residents of a system that measures time in eons.

Less concretely, it just feels wrong. Without large predators, wouldn't the woods seem less deep and shadowed, more like a theme park? We evolved huddled around a sheltering fire. What will we become without the primal fear that drove us to that ring of light? And if we kill the cougars, won't we also be admitting

Photo courtesy of Howard Copenhaver

Hunters made a lucrative wage off predator hatred in the bounty era, which began in colonial times and ended in the mid-twentieth century.

defeat, the defeat of the small-minded conqueror who destroys what he cannot appreciate or sustain?

Those of us who claim a right to live or play in cougar country must shoulder most of the responsibility for the choice: Do we want a safe world where we need not modify our behavior, or a more challenging world large enough for predators like cougars?

Modern environmentalism is all about preserving this larger world, but environmental activists won't have fully embraced their own ethic until mass mailings ask for more than money. In the twenty-first century, environmentalism's defining question will be, What will you give up for this big world? Time, land, freedom? Your easy myths? How about your life? Dollars are no longer—and never really were—enough.

Sources

A book like this requires picking the brains of hundreds of people. Those below were particularly generous with their time, expertise, and, in many cases, their painful memories. To the extent that we captured an accurate picture of coexistence with cougars, credit goes to them; any mistakes are ours.

Key witnesses and sources helped bring the stories in this book to life. They are Dave O'Keefe; Jim Mepham; Shane Duncan; Mike and Marie Smith; Gold River residents Suzanne Trevis, Ingrid Dahl, Carol Volk, Denise Watt, Barb Jackson, Cynthia Montgomery, Dale Frame, Bonnie and Chelsea Bellwood, Doug Kennedy, Peter Skilton, Dan McInnes, *Gold River Record* editor Jerry West, and Gold River Mayor Anne Fiddick; Port Alberni residents Bill Brown, Ron and Heather Receveur, Norm Nelson, and *Alberni Valley Times* editor Karen Beck; Karen Hanna, Jim and Karen Manion; Russ Bravard and Ernie Flores; Lucy Oberlin; Lona Kottle; Chuck and Cindy Traisi of Fund for Animals; Aaron Hall; Lila Lifely; Steve Carmichael; Christina Kafka; Richard Staskus; Tim Loewen and David Woodward of Victoria,

British Columbia's Empress Hotel; and Craig Grebicki.

Cougar hunters and trackers shared their intimate knowledge of cougars. They are Montanans Tom and Mel Parker, Tiger Hulett, Doug Caltrider, Ed Roche, Howard Copenhaver, Bob Sheppard, Bud Martin, and Bob Wiesner; Steve and Ann Ryan of Idaho; Dan Lay of British Columbia; Dave Fjelline of California; Lyle Wilmarth of Colorado; and Frank Smith of New Mexico.

Game managers, researchers, and wildlife enforcement officers shared their perspectives and experience. They are California Fish and Game Lt. Bob Turner; Washington Department of Fish and Wildlife Sgt. Ray Kahler; Laura Itogawa, supervising ranger, Cuyamaca Rancho State Park; Montana problem wildlife expert Eric Wenum; researchers Paul Beier, Dave Choate, Jim Halfpenny, David Shackleton, Maurice Hornocker, Toni Ruth, Kenny Logan, and Linda Sweanor; John Phelps of Arizona Department of Fish and Game; Steven Torres of California Department of Fish and Game; Todd Malmsbury and Anna Bazquez of the Colorado Division of Wildlife; Doug Caldwell of Rocky Mountain National Park; Jon Rachael and Mark Drew of Idaho Department of Fish and Game and Idaho Wildlife Health Laboratory, respectively; Rich DeSimone of Montana Department of Fish, Wildlife, and Parks; San Juan Stiver of Nevada Department of Game and Fish; Chuck Hayes of New Mexico Department of Game and Fish; Don Whittaker of Oregon Department of Fish and Wildlife; Paul B. Robertson and Raymond Skiles of Texas Parks and Wildlife and Big Bend National Park, respectively; Bill Bates and Steve Cranney of Utah Division of Wildlife Resources; Washington Department of Fish and Wildlife's Steve Pozzanghera, Sean Carrell, Margaret Ainscough, Madonna Luer, and Jim Rieck; Dave Moody of Wyoming Game and Fish Department; Bruce Treichel and Drew Mahaffey of Alberta Ministry of Environment; Matt Austin and Doug Janz of British Columbia Ministry of Environment; British Columbia conservation officers Lance Sundquist, Jerry Brunham, Pat Brown Clayton, and Bob Smirl; British Columbia Royal Canadian Mounted Police officer

Bill Bellwood; Walter Howard; California game wardens Bob Pirtle, Sean Pirtle, and Bob Teagle; California park rangers Stan Banksen and Donna Krucki; California park administrators Mark Jorgensen, Tim Miller, and Jim Burke; Lynn Sadler of the Mountain Lion Foundation in California; and U.S. Department of Agriculture Wildlife Services officer Jeff Brent.

Attack victims and their families deserve special note. They agreed to delve into difficult memories, usually out of a desire to teach people the truth about living among cougars. We hope this book honors their trust. Thanks go to Bill White and his family; the Parolin family, including Cindy's mother, Garnet Parker; the Schoener family; Kyle Musselman and his family; the Small family; the Mellon family; the survivors of Iris Kenna; Marv Waanders, uncle to Mark Miedema; Jason Underdahl and his family; Joel Anderson and his family; Dante Swallow and his family; and Johnny Wilson and his family.

Bibliography

Books and documents that informed our thinking include but are not limited to the following:

Aune, Keith. "Lion Report 98." CD-ROM presentation by author, Helena, Montana, 1998.

Barrett, Reginald and Paul Beier. *The Cougar in the Santa Ana Mountain Range, California.* Final report of the Orange County Cooperative Mountain Lion Study. University of California, Berkeley, 1993.

Beier, Paul. "Cougar Attacks on Humans in the United States and Canada." *Wildlife Society Bulletin* vol 19, no. 4 (1991).

————. "Cougar Attacks on Humans: An Update and some Further Reflections." Proceedings of the Fifteenth Vertebrate Pest Conference, University of California, Davis, 1992.

————. "Determining Minimum Habitat Areas and Habitat Corridors for Cougars." *Conservation Biology* vol 7, no. 1 (1993).

————. "A Checklist for Evaluating Impacts to Wildlife Movement Corridors." *Wildlife Society Bulletin* vol 20, no. 4 (1992).

————. "Dispersal of Juvenile Cougars in Fragmented Habitat." *Journal of Wildlife Management* vol 59, no. 2 (1995).

Beier, Paul with Dave Choate and Reginald Barrett. "Movement Patterns of Mountain Lions During Different Behaviors." *Journal of Mammalogy* vol 76, no. 4 (1995).

Bolgiano, Chris. *Mountain Lion: An Unnatural History of Pumas and People.* Pennsylvania: Stackpole Books, 1995.

Busch, Robert. *The Cougar Almanac: A Complete Natural History of the Mountain Lion.* New York: Lyons and Burford, 1996.

California Department of Fish and Game. *Lion-Human Interactions Reported on or Near Department Managed Lands.* Sacramento, 1998.

California Department of Fish and Game. *Outdoor California* (Sacramento), vol 57, no. 3. , (1995).

California Department of Fish and Game. *Report to the Senate Natural Resources and Wildlife Committee and the Assembly Water, Parks, and Wildlife Committee Regarding Mountain Lions.* Sacramento, 1994.

Colorado Division of Wildlife. "Mountain Lion-Human Interaction." Proceedings of symposium and workshop sponsored by the Colorado Division of Wildlife, 1991.

Danz, Harold. *Cougar!* Athens: Ohio University Press, 1999.

Hansen, Kevin. *Cougar, the American Lion.* Flagstaff: Northland Publishing Co., 1992.

Herrero, Stephen. *Bear Attacks: Their Causes and Avoidance.* New York: The Lyons Press, 1988.

Kerasote. *Bloodties: Nature, Culture, and the Hunt.* New York: Kodansha International, 1993.

Lassila, Kathrin Day. "The New Suburbanites." *The Amicus Journal* vol 21, no. 2 (1999).

Logan, Kenneth and Linda Sweanor. "Puma." Unpublished.

————. "The Cougars of New Mexico, Balancing the Needs of Cougars and People." *New Mexico Wildlife* (May/June 1997).

Mansfield, Terry and Richard Weaver. "The Status of Mountain Lions in California." Transactions of the Western Section of the Wildlife Society 25: 72-76, 1989.

Montana Fish, Wildlife, and Parks. *Management of Mountain Lions in Montana.* Final Environmental Impact Statement. Helena, 1996.

Montana Fish, Wildlife, and Parks. "Mountain Lions in Montana: A Survey of Montanans' Views." Helena, 1997.

Nelson, Richard. *Heart and Blood: Living With Deer in America.* New York: Alfred A. Knopf, 1997.

Olsen, Jack. *Night of the Grizzlies.* Moose, Wyoming: Homestead Publishing, 1996.

Padley, W. Douglas, ed. *Proceedings of the Fifth Mountain Lion Workshop.* Fort Collins, CO: Southern California Chapter of the Wildlife Society, 1996.

Ruth, Toni. "Mountain Lion Use of an Area of High Recreation Development in Big Bend National Park, Texas." Master's thesis, Texas A & M University, 1991.

Seidensticker, John, with Susan Lumpkin. "Mountain Lions Don't Stalk People. True or False?" *Smithsonian* vol 22 (February 1992).

Shaw, Harley. *Soul Among Lions.* Boulder: Johnson Books, 1989.

Torres, Steve. *Mountain Lion Alert: Safety Tips for Yourself, Your Children, Your Pets and Your Livestock in Lion Country.* Helena: Falcon, 1997.

Tischendorf, Jay and Steven Ropski, eds. *Proceedings of the Eastern Cougar Conference.* Erie: American Ecological Research Institute, 1994.

Torres, Steve et al. "Mountain Lion and human activity in California: testing speculations." Wildlife Society Bulletin, 1996.

Turner, Robert. "History of Mountain Lions Killed in San Diego County Since 1981." Lecture notes, 1999.

Index

cougar repellant, 26-27, 55,
153, 156
the effects of groups, 191
most effective actions, 192,
196
Sanders, Michael, 75
Schoener
Andrew, 12, 22
Barbara, xi, 197
cougar hunt, 19-23
initial search by friends, 1-7
memorial plaque, 9
murder evidence, 11-19
Pete, 2, 12, 22
Shackleton, David, 38
Shaw, Harley, 64
Sheppard, Bob, 176
Shields, Diane, 151-62
Size, 10-11
Small
David, 86, 87
Don, 86, 87
Laura, 85-88, 90, 91-92, 95
Sue, 85-88
Smirl, Bob, 36-37
Smith
Bruce, 83
Charles, 93
Frank, 62, 70, 71
Snares, 62, 71, 98
Soule, Karen, 119-36
Sources, 205-7
South Dakota, Rapid City, 103-4
Stalking behavior, 173-87
Staskus, Richard, 90

Stevan, Karen, 34-35
Survival rate, 99, 100
Swallow, Dante, 106, 191, 194
Sweanor, Linda, 59-61, 64, 70,
71, 72, 149
Swimming ability, 38

T

Tahsis Paper Company, 51-52
Texas
attacks 1951-1999, x
bounty hunting policy, 63
Torno, Steve, 26, 27, 28, 29, 31
Torres, Steve, 102, 190
Tracking. See Radio telemetry
Tracks, 173, 179
Tranquilizer darts, 37, 60, 80
Turner, Bob, 139, 142, 143, 145-
49, 161

U

Underdahl
Hazel, 104
Jason, 104
Judy, 103-4
Pete, 103, 104
United States
attack statistics, 40
attacks 1951-1999, ix-xi
United States. Fish and Wildlife
Service, 149
University of British Columbia,
38
Urban areas, 33, 35-38, 39,
73-83

About the Authors

Dean Miller is Managing Editor of the *Post Register* of Idaho Falls, Idaho, which has won regional awards for reportage on conservation and social issues and shared the 1998 National Batten Award for civic journalism. Formerly an award-winning reporter himself, Miller speaks at National Writers' Workshops about small town newspaper writing.

Jo Deurbrouck writes about adventuring, sports, travel and nature for magazines and newspapers. She lives with her husband and two dogs in rural Idaho. This is her second book.